A Visionary Life

By the Author

Visionary Business

How to Think Like a Millionaire
(with Mark Fisher)

A Two-Second Love Affair (Poetry)

Edited by the Author

As You Think by James Allen

The Art of True Healing by Israel Regardie

The Message of a Master by John McDonald

The Gift of Sobriety

Audio Cassettes

Visionary Business

Stress Reduction & Creative Meditations

Music

Solo Flight

Breathe

Petals

A
Visionary
Life

Conversations on
Personal and
Planetary Evolution

MARC ALLEN

New World Library
Novato, California

New World Library
14 Pamaron Way
Novato, California 94949

Cover design: Alexandra Honig
Cover photo: Ruriko Murakami / Photonica
Text design: Aaron Kenedi

Library of Congress Cataloging-in-Publication Data

Allen, Mark, 1946–
A visionary life : conversations on personal and planetary evolution
p.   cm.
ISBN 978-1-57731-021-1 (pbk.   :   alk. paper)
1. Conduct of life. 2. Success. I. Title
BJ1597.A45 1997   97-39586
158.1—dc21   CIP

First printing, February 1998
ISBN 978-1-57731-021-1

10   9   8   7   6   5   4   3

This book is dedicated to you,
with the wish and prayer that you
find something of lasting value
in its pages.

And dedicated to three writers who have given us
blueprints for the future:

To Buckminster Fuller,
for envisioning the possibility
of "a world with a steadily rising
standard of living for all,"
in a way that is entirely harmonious with all life
on our "Spaceship Earth."

To Barbara Marx Hubbard,
for writing Conscious Evolution,
and showing us the next step —
"becoming a universal humanity,
co-evolutionary with nature, and
co-creative with spirit."

To Riane Eisler,
for writing The Chalice and the Blade,
and showing us the possibility of a world
where partnership, rather than domination,
rules once more.

CONTENTS

A
Visionary
Life

Mind is the master power that molds and makes,
And we are Mind, and evermore we take
The tool of thought, and shaping what we will,
Bring forth a thousand joys, a thousand ills.
We think in secret, and it comes to pass —
Our world is but our looking glass.

— James Allen, *As You Think*

KEYS TO TRANSFORMING
YOUR LIFE AND THE WORLD

To live your life in your own way
To reach the goals you've set for yourself
To be the person you want to be
— that is success.

— (Author unknown)

A year had passed since the day an old man named Bernie walked into my struggling little business and shook my hand. I didn't know it then, but when I met Bernie I met my mentor.

A lot had happened over the year — I even had a book's worth of notes from conversations with Bernie on creating a visionary business. Along the way, I had come to understand how to create a successful business — at least theoretically — and I was beginning to see some convincing results from try-ing to practice what Bernie preached.

Whenever things would feel overwhelming, I would leaf through the pile of notes, and usually find something useful, even inspiring. At first I titled the notes *Meetings with a Remarkable Man*. Then it became *Visionary Business*.

I was flipping through the notes late one afternoon in the office when the phone rang.

"Still at it, eh?"

I recognized the soft old voice right away.

"Bernie — good to hear from you."

"What are you up to?"

"Well, I was just looking through some of my notes here. I've been thinking about organizing them in some way, and making you a copy."

"Interesting — that's just what I called about."

"My notes?"

"Yeah — and *my* notes, too. I've got a pile of them I'd like to talk to you about."

This sounded interesting.

"Want to come over, say, Saturday afternoon?" he said. "I've got an idea for you."

I had been to Bernie's house just a few times. It was on several acres of land bordering a national park, with miles of wilderness.

He met me at the door and offered me a cup of strong coffee. We took our steaming cups and went out about twenty or thirty yards behind his home, overlooking grassy meadows framed by pine-covered hills and winter fog.

He offered me an old weathered chair, solid and comfortable, and then disappeared back into the house. The chairs faced the south; the sun was warm on my face, even though it was mid-February. I took my jacket off and rolled up my shirt sleeves. Five minutes or so passed while I sipped coffee and listened to some noisy squawking bluejays chasing each other through the trees.

Bernie finally reappeared with an old shoe box under his arm, originally for cowboy boots. He handed it to me without saying a word. It was three-quarters filled with envelopes, napkins, pages torn from small notebooks, and typing paper, all covered with handwriting that went from small and neat to sprawling and sloppy.

"I've got all these notes," he said. "Years and years of notes, on creating the life you want — not just a visionary business, but a visionary *life*.

"It's completely unorganized — except maybe for this...." He leafed through the jumble of odd-shaped papers. "It's near the top somewhere... let me see....

"Here it is!" He held up a single sheet of paper. "Here's a way to organize it all, I think. Most of this stuff fits within these ten keys. Principles — and *practices*. Ideas and *actions*." He stood in front of me, like a comical, crazed professor.

"I've realized over the years I can *teach* someone — almost anyone, in fact, if they're interested — to be a visionary. It was something I learned, slowly, over many years. There are no *secrets of success* — but there are *keys* to it that can be learned. There are specific practices — *actions* — I can show you that can teach you how to change your life, and even the world, eventually. And that's the long-term project in all of this: personal and *planetary* evolution."

He sat down and was quiet for a moment, while I flipped through the notes. Some were barely legible. Some of it was poetry. Sometimes there was a single sentence on a page, or even a sentence fragment.

"Could you help me out with this?" he asked. He sounded like a plaintive five year old.

"What do you want me to do?"

"I've got all these ideas, but I just never get around to sitting down and organizing them. Could you do that for me? Type 'em up, make something out of them?"

He said it casually, as if it were no big deal, something I could toss off over a weekend, perhaps. I felt a wave of mixed emotions; it was a big project, it would take months. And I didn't know if I could pull all those scraps of paper into something coherent.

Yet the notes were fascinating; some were enigmatic, some beautiful, some illegible.

"I don't know, Bernie. It'd be quite a challenge to pull this together . . . it'd probably be kind of a mess."

"No more of a mess than it is right now," he said.

"Well, true."

I spent many evenings and weekends over the next few months trying to cobble his notes into some kind of rough form. I took ten file folders and labeled each with one of the keys. I tried to sort every single note into one of them. But it was impossible; most of the notes ended up in the "Uncertain" pile. It felt like it would be a huge, disjointed monster — if it ever got written.

As I typed it all up, though, I began to see the scope of Bernie's thinking. He had assembled, over the years, a list of ten keys — each was a principle and a *practice* as well — enough ideas and actions to create a complete course in self-actualization, to use Maslow's term. A course in mastery, in fulfillment. A course in real magic, if you will, *practical* magic. A course in how to create what you want in life — including no less than the conscious evolution of the whole world into a sustainable system with a steadily improving quality of life for all.

Bernie had summed it all up for me the night he gave me the box of notes. We had been sitting quietly, watching clusters of little clouds near the horizon turn into sparkling pink jewels set in a brilliant band of blue sky.

Then he said, "You know, we're *all* magicians. I've absolutely come to believe that, because I've seen it's true. We're all creative geniuses, in our own way, and we all have personal power. But most of us use our magical power to barely create enough money to pay the rent! Most of us barely create what we *need* — but not what we *want*.

"As soon as I started doing a few of these practices, my life started changing in all kinds of ways — ways I'd barely dared to dream about before."

We sat quietly for a moment.

"After all, Jesus said, *Ask and you shall receive.* He didn't say, *Ask and you shall receive, if you deserve it.* We all deserve it — we all deserve to live wonderful lives, fulfilling lives. That's what we want for our children, isn't it? We want them to be happy and fulfilled, to create what they want in their lives. If we wish that for our children, why don't we wish it for ourselves? And if we wish it for ourselves, it can come true.

"If you're not ready to hear this, or if it just isn't part of your particular path, I'll probably sound like a pompous old ass, or a goofball, and you won't even be able to hear what I'm saying. But if you're ready, you'll hear, and you'll understand. And your life will change, dramatically, for the better.

"You'll become a far more effective magician."

Bernie's words had been inspiring, but the work on the notes was frustrating. There were so many possibilities for the material, so many choices, different ways to organize it.

Finally I decided just to string together a possible rough draft for the first chapter. I worked late for several nights in a row before I had a pile of notes in a possible sequence. It lacked any connecting tissue, but it was a start.

Bernie called me the next day and invited me out to his home to read it. He wasn't in a hurry — I've never seen Bernie in a hurry for anything — but he was definitely enthusiastic about seeing it. I said I'd drive out right after work.

It was twilight when I arrived, blustery and cool. He offered me some hot tea, a blend of peppermint and other things, and we sat in front of a warm fire in his living room.

He was as smooth and serene as usual. I felt young, foolish, and agitated. He took off his shoes and sat like a kid, or a relaxed yogi, with his legs crossed on a big chair.

We stared at the fire for a while. Then Bernie said, "Okay, entertain me."

He closed his eyes and waited. I fumbled with the papers in the file folder, cleared my throat, sipped my tea, and began:

"Step one: *Imagine your ideal scene.*

"One of the most important keys to attaining success is knowing that *success is whatever you define it to be.*

"*To live your life in your own way, to reach the goals you've set for yourself, to be the person you want to be — that is success.* Whoever wrote that was a person of wisdom, and vision."

I had to clear my throat again. Bernie was perfectly still. I sipped my tea and went on.

"You have the ability to create the life *you* want, the life that embodies your deepest dreams and fantasies, and your highest aspirations. This is not necessarily the life your parents or your friends want for you, or your partner wants for you, or even the life you think you *should* have, because it is safe, secure, and sensible. It is the life of your dreams, whatever they may be. It may include a lot of changes — many people, over the course of a lifetime, will have several different careers and passions they want to pursue. Dreams can easily change over time.

"Take some time to consider what *you* want to create in your life. It will be time well spent. Take time to dream, to fantasize, and to eventually develop a plan, a *mental map*, that will lead you where you want to go."

I stopped reading; my throat was dry. Bernie looked at me with a calm gaze that was, for some reason, unsettling, even embarrassing. I shrugged my shoulders.

"Here, let me have a look at it," he said.

He spent several minutes reading through it, without saying a word, staring into the fire occasionally. Then he gave me that gaze again.

"You've done a lot — we've got something here."

I felt a wave of relief.

He spent another minute or so rummaging through all the notes in the box, reading a few at random.

"It's a good start. But it lacks something. I'm not sure what.... Pizazz — it lacks pizazz."

We sat in silence. Bernie stared at the fire.

"Here's what we'll do..." He got up and put my notes into the shoe box with all his other notes. He touched it to his forehead, then held it out in front of him.

"This is better," he said, and he threw the box into the blazing fire.

"Wait a second!" I shouted.

"No, this is better," he said quietly, as he watched the flames attack the paper. He was smiling, even chuckling, as he spoke.

"We'll start fresh. Let's just meet, over the next few months or so, and focus on one key at a time. You take notes, or record it, or whatever. I've got it all here in my head. The rest is just scribbling. Or typing. *Word processing.*"

He seemed to think the phrase was funny.

I stared at the fire as the box, and all those notes, were charred black and then turned into a weightless gray pile of ashes.

"Can you come over, oh . . . next Saturday?" Bernie asked. He was far more cheerful than I was.

KEY ONE

Imagine Your Ideal Scene

You will become as great as your dominant aspiration. . . . If you cherish a vision, a lofty ideal in your heart, you will realize it.

— James Allen, *As You Think*

The drive out to Bernie's place was beautiful, any time of year, through rolling hills dotted with oak trees and valleys of dense, silent forests of pine. It was especially stunning in the lush change of seasons, as winter turned into spring. I saw three waterfalls I had never seen before.

It was late morning when I arrived. He was having what he called breakfast — a blend of orange, mango, and grape-fruit juice. It was delicious. He poured us both a cup of strong coffee and we headed out behind his house and sat where we had before, overlooking the endless hills.

Bernie examined the little battery-operated tape recorder I brought along, and said it was "nifty." I hoped it wouldn't mess up. I felt some anxiety as I fumbled with a new tape, but Bernie seemed supremely relaxed about it all.

After I turned it on, he paused for a long time. It was clear there would be a lot of silence on the tape.

"It's always best, before we start something like this, to relax and do a short meditation. Before any kind of study, any classes or talks, even just a bit of quiet meditation helps us absorb the words much more deeply.

"Put the recorder down for a minute."

And he guided me through an exercise, doing it himself as well, almost whispering at times.

AN EXERCISE AT THE BEGINNING

"Sit comfortably; relax your arms, relax your hands in your lap, close your eyes. Take a slow, deep breath. As you exhale slowly, *relax your body....* Take another deep breath. As you exhale slowly, *relax your mind....* Take another breath. As you exhale slowly, *let everything go,* let yourself feel totally relaxed....

"Just enjoy the feeling for a moment, breathing softly. It feels so good to simply relax....

"Now just tell yourself you're ready to absorb, easily and effortlessly, everything that's necessary for you... to grow, to expand, to evolve. To reach your objectives, to create the life you want, the world you want. There is something valuable here for you, at this moment, and you intuitively know what it is.

"Repeat to yourself, *I am now, easily and effortlessly, absorbing everything I need.... I am now, easily and effortlessly, achieving my dreams and goals.... I am now, easily and effortlessly, creating the life I want....*

"Take a few more deep breaths, and notice how good those words feel — or change them, if better ones come to mind! Now you're ready.

"Take one last deep breath and open your eyes, refreshed and relaxed, ready, willing, and able to fully be the magician and creative genius you already are... ready, willing, and able to change your life for the better, in any way you desire."

We opened our eyes. The world sparkled. Bernie sat quietly for a moment before he spoke.

"I'm offering *only one option* with these keys. Take them and work with them and develop other options for yourself. Use only words that resonate positively and powerfully for you. Change any of the words I say, or any of the exercises I give you, to make them work for you. Each of us is unique — and we intuitively know what's most effective for us.

"This kind of meditation gives instructions, programming, to your subconscious mind. Your subconscious is infinitely powerful — it knows no limits, only those you impose on it through your own limiting thoughts and beliefs.

"Meditation like this opens you up, intuitively. Even if it has no other noticeable effect than to help you relax for a minute or two, it's certainly worthwhile."

UNDERSTANDING, KNOWLEDGE, AND WISDOM

"I want to say one more thing right at the start — something I was taught by a Tibetan Buddhist teacher named Tarthang Tulku. It's taught to all students at the beginning of their instruction.

"There are three distinct stages to worthwhile learning:

"First, we have to hear or read the information, and we have to understand it. To do this, we need to be open and receptive. Our minds have to be relatively quiet, and we have to be willing to listen and hear.

"In the second stage, we reflect on the information, so that we relate to it personally, and assimilate it into our own experience. At this stage, we not only understand it but see its truth in our lives — and *understanding becomes knowledge.*

"Finally, we have to *live* this knowledge fully, embody it, and practice it every moment of our lives. The words penetrate to our hearts, to our subconscious minds. The words then have power to affect our life experience. At this stage, *knowledge becomes wisdom.*"

He sat in silence for a moment. Nearby, a crow landed on the topmost branch of a young pine tree and bounced and squawked hoarsely three times, adding exclamation points to Bernie's words.

THE KEY TO THE PROCESS IN A NUTSHELL

Bernie spoke the next words slowly and forcefully.

"Everything we've created in our lives was first a thought, and then a feeling. When a thought and feeling are combined and held onto, it results in a focused vision, and finally manifests as something tangible.

"We're all creative beings, creating everything we have in our lives, at every moment, for better or worse. Some people use their creative energy for success, some for failure. Some create works of art, some destroy what others create. Some create a mansion on a hill, some create a bottle of cheap fortified wine on the meanest streets in town.

"Everything we do is a creative act — something that requires its own planning — and is the result of some kind of vision."

We sat in silence and reflected on those words for a few minutes; then he smiled broadly.

"We've got to open the book with a poem — just like traditional Tibetan Buddhist books. The tradition says if you understand the poem, you don't need to read the book, because all the wisdom in the book is contained in the poem."

He was as exuberant as a child.

"James Allen said it all in the poem that opens his great book, *As You Think.*"

He quoted, forcefully, from memory:

"Mind is the master power that molds and makes,
And we are mind, and evermore we take

The tool of thought, and shaping what we will,
Bring forth a thousand joys, a thousand ills.
We think in secret and it comes to pass —
Our world is but our looking glass."

We sat in silence again. Everything was calm and quiet.

CREATING YOUR IDEAL SCENE

"The first key isn't all that difficult to understand — it's even kind of fun to do. And it's the single most important thing you can do in your life, because it leads to all the other keys. It even *contains* all the other keys, if it's done fully enough.

"The first key is to *imagine your ideal scene.*"

The First Key:
Clearly imagine your ideal scene;
write it down on paper,
and keep reviewing it.

"Imagine five years have passed — or two years, if you're impatient, or ten, if you're patient. In those years, you were so inspired by these words" — Bernie had to laugh at this — "and by everything else that's inspired you along the way — that *everything* has happened to you in the best way you can imagine. You've created your dreams; you've become a success, in every way you can imagine, in everything you most desire. Best of all, it's happened in an easy and relaxed manner, in a healthy and positive way.

"What will you be doing, *ideally?* What have you accomplished? Where will you be living? What does your home look like? What are your relationships like? What's a typical day for you? What are you doing to contribute to a better world?

"Just let your imagination go. Be as farfetched as possible. Shoot for the moon! Let it be *ideal* — we'll deal with reality later.

"Be sure to write it down. Don't worry that writing will make it too concrete — it isn't carved in stone; you can always change it later, if you want. Just play with it, have fun with it. Don't worry that it's too big a dream; we'll deal with doubts and limiting beliefs — and detachment — later.

"Take a sheet of paper and write MY IDEAL SCENE at the top. Suspend your doubts and limitations and let your imagination soar.

"After you've written it, find a special folder or notebook — or even a beautiful box or something — and put it in there. We'll add more to it later. This is the beginning, the essential first step, in creating what you want in life.

"Keep reviewing your ideal scene, so you keep it in mind. This is the most important work you can do. It's your visualization of your future. It's the first part of your map to success — no matter what you define that success to be."

He sipped his coffee and looked off into the distance. There was another long beat of silence.

"I'm not exaggerating when I say this little exercise was probably the single most important thing I ever did in my life. I remember it vividly. It was the day of my thirtieth birthday, the most difficult — and the best — single day I've ever had. I spent most of the day pacing back and forth in my little slum apartment, taking a good look at my life. I was in an odd state of shock. I realized I wasn't a kid anymore; yet I felt so young, so unprepared.

"I looked at my strengths and weaknesses, and I was honest with myself in a way I'd never been before.

"I'd always done what I was passionate about, without compromising. That was a strength, something I was born with, something a lot of people learn only with difficulty, or never learn at all. And it's *essential* to real success, and fulfillment.

"I'd done a lot of interesting things in my twenties. I went to Europe and India. I met all kinds of fascinating people, saw other cultures, religions, studied other philosophies. I learned about meditation, and that's been invaluable to me all my life. I recommend meditation to *everyone.*

"I'd attained at least some degree of peace, a bit of serenity, at times, because of the meditation I'd done — and yet my thirtieth birthday was tough emotionally. After thirty years of life, I was an *adult*. It was undeniable. And I'd accomplished very little. I had no job, no income, no assets, no committed relationship. Worst of all, I had no direction, no goals. I didn't know where I wanted to go in life — and so of course I was going nowhere. I didn't have a clue about how to attain success. I'd never even taken the first step of defining what success meant for me — what I wanted to do with my life!

"For thirty years, I'd been a follower, not a leader. I'd followed teachers in school, girlfriends and gurus and other people after school. And I'd been left with nothing, at least materially. Spiritually, mentally, and emotionally, the meditation I was doing had good effects — but it didn't help pay the rent. It was time for me to *somehow* start directing the course of my life.

"I remembered a game I'd played, years earlier, with a group of friends. I didn't remember what I'd said in the game when I first played it. I wasn't ready, obviously, to understand its value. I didn't realize it was a key to success. But the day I turned thirty, something in me shifted. I played the game, all alone, pacing up and down in my funky little apartment. My cat thought I'd gone nuts.

"I pretended five years had passed, and everything had gone as well as I could possibly imagine....

"A picture immediately sprang to mind: I owned my own business! I owned a beautiful hotel, a place of rejuvenation and peace and pleasure. It was highly successful, and I was able to invest in all kinds of other businesses, and support all kinds of people in reaching their dreams. I supported my employees through profit-sharing, and contributed abundantly to a great many nonprofit groups doing good work in the world, taking care of people, and the environment. I had a loving wife and a family. I owned a beautiful home, in a quiet, peaceful place, surrounded by open land...."

He gestured around as he said it.

"And best of all, I was doing it *in an easy and relaxed manner, in a healthy and positive way, in its own perfect time.* That was my ideal.

"This picture — this *vision* — felt so good. Even just dreaming of it was empowering to me in some way. *Instantly.*

"But as soon as it sprang to mind, a *flood* of doubts and fears sprang up as well. Voices cried out, *It's way too much. It won't work. You're asking for trouble, for failure. You'll never be able to do it all. You don't have what it takes. Pick something smaller and safer to do with your life, something easier to achieve.*

"But I'd done enough meditation, and learned enough to know those inner voices were agitated and apprehensive — so I knew they were the voices of my fears, of my limiting beliefs. As soon as I recognized that, another voice spoke, calmer and clearer and I knew it was my intuition, my inner guidance. I'd learned to identify it: It always speaks confidently. It always speaks the truth. It's calm and quiet. It always feels right.

"That voice said, *Don't listen to your doubts and fears. They'll dissolve, over time, because they're not true. The truth is, you can have whatever you can dream of. There are no limits to what you can accomplish, if you follow your intuition, and find your vocation, your calling, and do what's aligned with your mission in life. You can accomplish great things — you can be as great as you can dream!*

"It's true for me, and it's true for you. It's true for everyone, if they understand this key — if they have the knowledge and courage to write down their ideal scene, and if they keep focused on the vision it always contains.

"I wrote it down, and have never forgotten it. It changed my life.

"It evolved over the years into a lifetime plan, not just a five-year plan. And it keeps evolving, growing. Now my ambition is no less than to carry on Buckminster Fuller's work, and Barbara Marx Hubbard's work, and Riane Eisler's work, and help the entire planet evolve into a system that works, a sustainable system that supports all life upon it. A world of peace and plenty for all, bringing back, and evolving into, the partnership model rather than the dominator model, to use Riane Eisler's words. But I'm getting ahead of myself — that's the final key, the *ten percent solution* we'll talk about later.

"One step at a time. We need to take care of ourselves before we can take care of others. We need to imagine how we can be fulfilled, how we can contribute to the world in a way no one else can. For we're all creative geniuses, I'm convinced of that — all we need are the right tools. All we need is the right understanding, the knowledge of our own capability and power.

"Creating an ideal scene leads to every other step, every other key. It teaches you how to be a visionary. Within your ideal scene is the vision of your success in the world, the vision of the world to come."

We sat in silence. A warm wind began to blow, and the trees waved their branches.

I went home and wrote down my ideal scene. It was scarier to do than I thought it would be. It was definitely a challenge. But it felt good to put all my vague, amorphous dreams into concrete words. I filled two handwritten pages, put them in a white folder, and put it in my top desk drawer.

I, too, wanted to create a successful business, and help to make the world a better place for all. I, too, wanted to own a beautiful home, and have a family, or at least a loving relationship. But a lot of doubts arose, in full force. My dreams were far from my current reality.

KEY TWO

Discover Your Vocation, and Your Mission or Purpose in Life

Until thought is linked with purpose, there is no intelligent accomplishment....

— James Allen, *As You Think*

Bernie called a few days later. He was going to be in town — my office, or his? It was a no-brainer — his office was far more comfortable than mine. It even had room service.

He had a suite in a downtown hotel, on the mezzanine floor, with a balcony in front, overlooking the lobby. We sat in comfortable stuffed chairs and watched the people come and go from our perch above. We had lunch delivered, and Bernie had his usual: a ham sandwich on white bread.

I told him I had written down my ideal scene, and it was surprisingly hard to do — scary, in fact.

"Oh, then I forgot to add one thing," he said. "At the top of your ideal scene, write, in big capital letters,

IN AN EASY AND RELAXED MANNER,

IN A HEALTHY AND POSITIVE WAY,

IN ITS OWN PERFECT TIME.

"Then write your ideal scene. Later, when we get to goals, you should do the same thing: always start your list with those words. Keep repeating them to yourself, until they sink into your subconscious. Before you know it, you'll be accomplishing everything you need *in an easy and relaxed manner, in a healthy and positive way, in its own perfect time.*"

When I thought about it, that was the way Bernie seemed to do everything. He never hurried; he always had plenty of time.

We finished our lunch, watching the people busily come and go.

"All right — I'm ready," he said. He smiled broadly. "You know, I'm really enjoying doing this with you. This is more fun than Christmas for me, it really is. Of course, I'm Jewish. But my wife's Catholic, so I still have fun at Christmas. This work you're doing — it's the best possible gift you could give me."

He said it in such a heartfelt way, with a radiance and pure joyfulness I had only seen before in little children. For some reason, a few tears welled up; I turned away to hide the softness in my eyes.

He pointed to the tape recorder. I turned it on, and he began.

"Think about your ideal scene. Imagine as vividly as you can that you're actually living it. Take a moment to enjoy how it feels. This kind of fantasy is healthy and lucrative, for within your ideal scene is a great deal of information about you — information that leads to knowledge and wisdom. And power.

"Within your ideal scene is your vocation, or calling. Don't just find a job — find your vocation.

"Vocation comes from the Latin word that means *calling*. Somewhere in your ideal scene, it's calling to you.

"And somewhere, if you reflect on it, your mission or purpose in life is calling, too. It's probably linked, in some way, with your vocation — though not necessarily.

"This is the next key."

The Second Key:
Discover your vocation,
and your mission or purpose in life,
and write them down as simply
and clearly as possible.

"Every one of us has a vocation and a mission or purpose in life that's absolutely unique, and it's up to each of us to discover what it is.

"Some of us are born knowing our vocation and our mission or purpose clearly. Some of us discover it early in life, some much later. Some find it easy to discover. Some have to dig deep, question long and hard, maybe take a long break from work or go on a quest of some kind before their vocation and purpose emerges.

"If you write down your ideal scene, your vocation and purpose will be somewhere on that page or in those pages. Your vocation will probably be obvious, but you might have to extend the vision of your ideal scene higher and greater to find your mission, your purpose in life — it's your ultimate reason for being, and you'll probably find it encompasses your entire ideal scene and even goes beyond it, into a great mission, a great purpose that has impact in the world.

"All of humanity, all the world, needs you and your great purpose. This is the unavoidable truth. You can deny it, but that doesn't mean it isn't true. You can fail to achieve your potential, but that doesn't mean you weren't destined for greatness — all it means is you settled for less than you could have been because you didn't reach for the stars."

He pulled a well-worn paperback book out of his suit coat pocket. "James Allen wrote beautifully about this key in *As You Think,* one of the greatest self-empowerment books of all time, a book I've read dozens of times.

"Let's see…." He flipped it open to the Contents page.

"Here it is — *Thought and Purpose:* [1]

"Until thought is linked with purpose there is no intelligent accomplishment. With most people, the bark of their thinking is allowed to drift upon the ocean of life. Aimlessness is a vice, and such drifting must not continue for those who would steer clear of catastrophe and destruction.

"Those who have no central purpose in their lives fall an easy prey to petty worries, fears, troubles, and self-pitying, all of which are indications of weakness, and which lead, just as surely as deliberately planned crimes (though by a different route), to failure, unhappiness, and loss, for weakness cannot persist in a power-evolving universe.

"We need to conceive of a legitimate purpose in our heart, and set out to accomplish it. We should make this purpose the centralizing point of our thoughts.

"It may take the form of a spiritual ideal, or it may be a material object, according to our nature at the time; but whichever it is, we should steadily focus our thought-forces upon the object we have set before ourselves. We should make this purpose our supreme duty, and devote ourselves to its attainment.

"Even if we fail again and again to accomplish our purpose — as we necessarily must until our weakness is overcome — the strength of character gained will be the measure of our true success, and this will form a new starting point for future power and triumph.

"These words are worth reflecting on. In a way, he combines the first five keys we're going to explore into one great key, uniting our dreams and purpose and goals and visualization into one powerful force.

"The purpose I suggest you focus on at this time is a bit different, though — it's much broader than any particular long-term goal, broader even than your ideal scene. It's the highest, most expansive purpose you can imagine, a great mission, a challenge that will last a lifetime. It can be stated simply, in few words — one sweeping sentence or paragraph is usually enough. It's very personal — it's yours alone, something to share with only your closest and most supportive friends.

"Take a sheet of paper, and put MY VOCATION, or even VOCATION — CALLING at the top. Then write whatever comes to mind. After that, write MY MISSION OR PURPOSE IN LIFE. Then write your mission, your purpose, in one paragraph. Put it in your folder or notebook with your ideal scene.

"It's an important part of your map to success, or your *power kit* — or whatever you want to call it — the most valuable folder you have. I keep mine in the top drawer of my dresser. I've written on the front, in large letters: *I am now creating the life I want.* And I've signed it with my name and affirmed it with my heart.

"And best of all, I've watched it come true. I now live my ideal scene. I have for many years. So, of course, I'm on to creating a new ideal scene, far more expansive than the others, though my purpose remains the same. A great purpose.

"By writing down your vocation and purpose or mission, you've taken another step to focus your creative energies in the highest and most effective way possible. You've taken another step to being a powerful person able to manifest your dreams.

"Powerful people have a calling. They know their purpose, their mission, in life."

We sat in silence for a while.

"That's it," Bernie said. "That's all that needs to be said."

I went straight home and wrote my vocation and mission down, and added it to my folder. It spilled out quickly; it was exciting.

Now my life has a purpose. Perhaps it was always there — but perhaps it would have remained hidden, and unfulfilled, if I hadn't taken the brief time it took to think about it, and write it down.

KEY THREE

Create Long-Term Goals — A Five-Year Plan that Will Evolve into a Lifetime Plan

Act as if it were impossible to fail.

— Dorothea Brande, *Wake Up and Live*

Bernie strolled into my office about a week later, late in the afternoon. I was in a rush of hurried business. It had been a long, strenuous day, phones ringing constantly. My desk was a paper-scattered wreck. I was losing things, important things. It had led to a major gaffe; I had forgotten to do something that was vitally important to that month's income. People were upset with me, and for good reason. I had messed up, and the whole company suffered for it. I was tired and jangled. And I had consumed far too much coffee; the last two cups just made me more sluggish.

Bernie ambled into my little office and caught me ending a harried, frustrating phone conversation. He sat in the chair in front of my desk and quietly waited, enveloped as usual in an aura of calmness, a slight smile on his face.

As soon as I hung up the phone, he said, "Years ago, I heard a great bit of advice I always try to remember: *Don't sweat the small stuff. And it's all small stuff.*"

He waited for my response. I felt like a little kid caught doing something obnoxious. I shrugged.

"I've got the perfect thing for you," he said. He pulled a little bag out of his pocket. "*Valerian tea.* Got a teapot?"

We went into the little kitchen area, and soon the tea was steaming. It smelled funky — a familiar smell, but I couldn't quite place it.

"It smells like dirty socks, I know, but it doesn't taste too bad," Bernie said. "And it's the most relaxing tea in the world. Perfect at the end of the day. Or any time you need to relieve stress."

We took it back to my office. "Every American, probably everyone in the so-called civilized world, could use some valerian tea now and then," he said. "It's a wonderful sedative, sort of an herbal valium. But more gentle, without the negative effects of valium."

After about half a cup, I swear I could feel my stress evaporating. Or maybe it was just being in Bernie's presence. It *was* all small stuff after all, when I thought about it.

"Ready for the next key?" he asked.

I was only too glad to quit thinking about the small stuff and hear what Bernie had to say. I closed the door and got out my tape recorder.

"All right — we've imagined our ideal scene, we've reflected on our vocation and our mission or purpose in life, and we've put it all down on paper. Now we're ready for the next key, one that's challenging and exciting: making a list of long-term goals.

"Within your ideal scene, when you think about it, are several important long-term goals — quite possibly, if you're thorough enough in imagining your ideal scene, *all* your long-term goals.

"Let's define long-term goals as anything that'll take over six months to accomplish. Or three months, or a year — whatever works for you. Maybe the best working definition is this: long-term goals are those you list and place in your folder, along with your ideal scene and purpose. Short-term goals are those you put into your daily calendar, and move toward on a daily or weekly basis."

He sat quietly for a moment, and sipped his tea.

EFFECTIVE LONG-TERM GOALS

"The most effective goals are clear and concise. Effective long-term goals have four qualities." He counted on his fingers.

"One: *Your goals should be measurable.* 'I am successful' is not the best way to phrase that goal; it's far too vague. What does success mean to you in measurable terms? 'I have an annual income of over $100,000' — that's measurable. You either attain it or you don't, so there's no question about it in your mind. Another possibility might be, 'I work at something I love, pay all my expenses easily and effortlessly, save at least ten percent of my income for my financial independence, and give at least ten percent to worthy causes.' Find your own words for your goals — just make sure they're measurable.

"Two: *Your goals should arise out of your own desire and be emotionally exciting for you.* The key to real fulfillment is to create the life *you* want, not the life someone else wants for you — not necessarily even the life you think you *should* have, to be safe and secure and sensible. What do you really want? If you could be, do, or have anything, what would it be?

"If the words 'billionaire rock star' leap to mind, for example, that's certainly a challenging goal. Even if you never achieve it, the life you create by reaching for it, stretching for it, will be fulfilling for you — *if* that goal also meets the other two conditions:

"Three: *Your goals and activities should be aligned with your ideal scene and your purpose in life.* If they're not, you're working against yourself, against the whole universe.

"Finally: *Your goals should in no way harm others.* This includes people, animals, and the environment. If what you do harms others, the effects of your actions eventually return to harm you, and you'll never be happy or fulfilled.

"*As you sow, so you shall reap* — it's the law of karma, and it's absolute."

> **The Third Key:**
> **Create long-term goals —**
> **at least a five-year plan — that will**
> **evolve in time into a lifetime plan.**
> **Read your goals out loud often**
> **to keep them in mind.**

"Take a sheet of paper — or go to your computer — and write or type at the top:

> **IN AN EASY AND RELAXED MANNER,**
> **IN A HEALTHY AND POSITIVE WAY,**
> **IN ITS OWN PERFECT TIME...**

"Then list every worthwhile long-term goal you can think of. Some might not take that long to accomplish, others might take years, even decades. A lifetime.

"You might want to end your list with this: *I live my ideal scene,* and then add a short version of your ideal scene.

"At the bottom, you can add the words:

SO BE IT. SO IT IS.

"You may or may not want to include this. I like it because it's strong and concrete, and has a powerful effect.

"We'll talk about adding one more thing to the very top of your list later, when we look at detachment. But this will do it for now.

"Read your list, preferably out loud, *at least once a day for at least twenty-one days,* and then as often as necessary to keep those goals implanted in your mind. Even if they seem almost impossible when you first write them down, eventually, your subconscious accepts them and you find yourself creating them, as if by magic. And it is magic — practical, *real* magic.

"When you've attained a goal, be sure to acknowledge your accomplishment and express your gratitude in some way, and cross it off your list. Rewrite your list every once in a while to keep it clean and current. I rewrite mine on New Year's Day, and sometimes again in midsummer."

He held his cup in his long fingers and stared into it for a while, without saying a word, as if he were divining something in the cup.

"If you make this list of your goals, it'll surprise you — you'll find it's very effective. I've often wondered *why;* here are at least some of the reasons:

"It keeps you focused on your goals; it keeps them in the

forefront of your consciousness. This puts your powerful subconscious mind to work and moves you toward those goals far more quickly than if they remain unstated and unaffirmed.

"It also helps you to expand and become a more creative person, simply by repeating the goals to yourself. If they're written clearly, it feels wonderful to repeat them. It's stimulating, emotionally and mentally. Part of you grows as a result. Subconsciously you expand in exactly the way that's necessary for you to fulfill your dreams.

"The simple act of reading your goals also helps dissolve doubts and fears, limiting beliefs and emotional blocks; it reinforces the fact that you are, in reality, a powerful, creative person.

"And repeating the phrase, *In an easy and relaxed manner, in a healthy and positive way, in its own perfect time* ... at the beginning of your goals has a great side effect: After reading your list for several days the words sink deeply into your subconscious mind. Before you know it, without conscious effort, things that would have been stressful in the past are resolved in an easy and relaxed manner. The words automatically come to mind, just when you need them, sometimes consciously, sometimes unconsciously, and you relax and open up to more possibilities, more opportunities. And you find it's much easier to do things in an easy and relaxed way than in a stressed-out way."

"I should have remembered that today," I said. "Today was tough."

"It's something we should all learn, and remember," Bernie said. "It makes life so much easier. But we forget, over and over. And we need to keep reminding ourselves, over and over.

"Repeat that phrase before you read your goals — and any time you can remember it throughout the day. Repeat it until your subconscious accepts it as absolute truth — until you've actually programmed yourself to do things *in an easy and relaxed manner, in a healthy and positive way.*"

I took another sip of valerian tea. I definitely felt more relaxed.

Bernie stared at his cup again, cradled in his hands. He sat in silence, motionless, either meditating or thinking deeply. When he spoke, his voice was quiet and deep.

"Some people have difficulty with the phrase, *in its own perfect time.* Effective goals, as we have seen, should be measurable, and one way to measure them is to set a specific deadline. When you have a goal of creating a specific annual income, for example, and then include the words *in its own perfect time,* isn't that a contradiction?

"It *is* a contradiction to your rational mind, but it doesn't seem to bother your subconscious mind. And if you don't reach your goal within a given time period, the phrase *in its own perfect time* is a reminder that things are unfolding with their own time schedule — and often it's beyond us, beyond our power to affect. Even though it's essential to make specific time lines, it's just as important not to get frustrated or, worse yet, defeated if those goals aren't reached as quickly as you'd like. The trick is to make clear goals, and yet be unattached to the results.

"We live and grow like every other plant and animal on the planet, according to nature's timetable. I look at all the young pines near my house, and realize we're a lot like they are. During a wet year, they burst upward with bright new growth. During a dry year, they hardly grow at all. Over time, over many years, they reach great heights. Their growth feels slow to us, but it's *inexorable*.

"Growth takes time, often more than our arbitrary goals give us. As Rilke wrote — in his great book *Letters to a Young Poet* — *ten years is nothing*. I often think of that. We live in a frenetic, work-oriented, even *workaholic* culture; many of us feel that looking even five years ahead is an impossibly long time. A year may seem like a long, long time away. Yet a year flies by so quickly, and if we're floating along aimlessly, we've accomplished nothing more to move us even one step toward any of our long-term goals and our ideal scene."

He contemplated his tea leaves again.

"Make definite dates for your long-term goals whenever possible. But don't feel defeated if you have to revise those dates, again and again. Your goals will be met in their own perfect time — and ten years is nothing, in your subconscious mind, and in the grander scheme of it all."

YOUR POWER KIT

"Write down your long-term goals, review them often,

and keep them with your ideal scene and your vocation and mission or purpose in life. These are the most essential elements in your folder, your personal power kit, or magician's tool kit, or whatever you want to call it.

"I have other things in my folder, that you may or may not want to add. And I'm sure, if you use it, you'll come up with other things as well. Here are some of the things I've had in my folder over the years:

"A summary of the steps of the *core belief process*, and a summary of the *communication process* — we'll get to those later.

"Pages of my journal that relate in some way to my ideal scene, vocation, purpose, or goals. If you write a journal, this is a good place to keep it.

"There are various inspiring quotes from writers and speakers I want to keep and remember. The best quote I came across recently, for instance, is from Dorothea Brande: *Act as if it were impossible to fail.* That's a great piece of advice! What would you do if you acted as if it were impossible to fail? How would you act? What would you do?

"I also keep various notes and affirmations that are meaningful. For years, I kept this affirmation in my notebook, and on the wall of my bedroom and office as well: *I am sensible and in control of my finances. I am creating total financial success, in an easy and relaxed manner, in a healthy and positive way, in its own perfect time.* After eight or ten years, that affirmation came true. Then I replaced it with a new one that'll last me for the rest of my life:

*"Miracles follow miracles
and wonders never cease,
for all my expectations
are for the good."*

We sat in silence. Then Bernie took his cup off his lap and set it carefully on my desk.

"That's it."

"That's good stuff, Bernie," I said. "If I want to get critical, though, I'd say maybe there's a bit too much repetition in it."

"Repetition? Repetition is essential!" Bernie said, with surprising vehemence. "We need repetition to replace the repetition of old habits! The more repetition the better! Most people just quickly read through a book once and think they understand it. Maybe that's okay for some kinds of books — but this needs repetition! So don't worry about it."

I had to chuckle. Then I thought of a question.

"So *all* of your long-term goals spring from your ideal scene?"

"Right. If your ideal scene is fully sketched out, it'll contain all your long-term goals. Your ideal scene is like the story boards a film director will have drawn before shooting a movie.

"Once I'd imagined my ideal scene, I saw my two main long-term goals were to start and build a successful business and to buy a beautiful home for a family. Those goals took me quite a while to achieve, of course. I had to break them down into achievable long-term steps. First I had to start a business, and I had to somehow find a way to get into a little starter home.

"With my goal to start a business, I realized, one, I had no money, and two, I knew nothing about business. So my first two steps were obvious to me: I needed to get a job, and save some money to finance my business, and I needed to learn more about business itself. So I found a perfectly awful job, working for a terrible boss, and I bought a used Business 101 textbook and read it. And those steps led me to the next ones.

"When I look back on it, I have to laugh about how naive I was. I knew nothing about business, nothing at all about financing, and so the only way I could think of to finance my business was to get a job and try to save some money. Later on, when I learned more about business, I saw there are many other ways to finance a business, or any other creative idea: loans, equity investors, limited partnerships — there are all kinds of creative ways to raise money. But I knew nothing about any of that. So I took the long, slow route, learning as I went.

"If I were to start another company knowing what I know now, I'd do a business plan and raise all the capital I need, easily and effortlessly. Because now I know there's no shortage of money out there — there are plenty of people with money to invest in your creative ideas. You just need to learn how to approach them. An article in *Forbes* magazine a while ago, in fact, claimed there's too much venture capital chasing too few good ideas! Can you imagine! That's the opinion of a lot of people with a lot of money. They don't know what to do with it. An entrepreneur's job is to find some people with money and show them an exciting investment opportunity. The first step is to write a good, solid business plan, and pass it around to everyone you can think of who knows anyone with any money.

"But I knew nothing about any this when I started. I never studied business in school. I learned, step by step, by doing it — I took the first obvious step in front of me, and that always led to the next step.

"And then there was my plan for a home. I knew, when I thought it through, that I'd probably need to think of buying *three* homes to get my dream home: First, a little starter house — anything at all where I would start building equity in something rather than paying rent. Then move up to a nicer home in a better neighborhood. Then my ultimate dream home, where I'll stay as long as I live.

"It took me about seven years after I did my ideal scene before I could afford my first starter home. It was literally the cheapest house in the whole county. Small and rectangular and right by the highway. But after eight years, it had nearly doubled in price, and I was able to sell it and use that equity for a down payment on a nice home in a quiet neighborhood. Eight years after that, I could afford to get my dream home. So it took me quite a few years, because I started with nothing. But I ended up achieving my long-term goal."

There was a moment of silence.

"It's a very satisfying feeling, one that never leaves you — the fulfillment of a dream held for a long time. And it's just as satisfying to teach others to fulfill their dreams too."

I thought about Bernie's beautiful home, and his yard with its inspiring views. I hoped I would remember his words. I hoped I wouldn't forget, and go back to old patterns of thought and old habits that led me nowhere.

Later that evening, I made a list of my long-term goals. I had some difficulty doing it. My goals were definitely ambitious, and I had some mixed feelings about that. *Ambition* was a word with negative connotations, when I thought about it. Ambitious people were egomaniacs who hurt other people on the way up. They were power-hungry, greedy, and selfish. But when I thought about those old beliefs, I realized they weren't necessarily true. To achieve my dreams, I definitely needed *great* ambition, for I was shooting for the stars, but that didn't mean I needed to hurt other people or be greedy and selfish. If I was truly successful, in fact, it meant I would have the resources to help a lot of other people as well.

As long as my goals were aligned with my purpose, I felt I wouldn't hurt others, or be greedy or selfish. Ambition doesn't have to have the negative connotations many of us attach to it. Ambition, and desire, are essential ingredients for success.

KEY FOUR

Create Short-Term Goals that Move You Toward Each Long-Term Goal

Within every desire is the seed and mechanics for its fulfillment.

— Deepak Chopra
The Seven Spiritual Laws of Success

I met Bernie at the hotel suite he called an office a few days later. He had his ham sandwich, and I had an excellent pasta dish. The first hour was filled with casual conversation. Bernie talked about a trip to Brazil he had taken with his Brazilian wife.

"Those people have a lot to teach us Americans," he said. "They know how to enjoy life. They're the party specialists of the planet."

I had to chuckle. Bernie had never mentioned his age, and I had never asked, but he was probably about seventy. I had never heard anyone his age talk the way he did.

"They know what's important in life. Friends, family, enjoying life. Celebrating every chance they get. We take things too seriously, especially our work. And money. Money is a means to an end, not an end in itself. So many people get so focused on chasing the almighty dollar they forget what's important in life.

"No one has *ever*, on their deathbed, wished they'd made more money."

He chuckled and picked up the phone and ordered a couple of cappuccinos.

"All right," he said. "Today we're discovering another key — one that becomes obvious once you write a list of long-term goals." He sat back comfortably in his chair and looked off into the distance above and beyond me.

"When you reflect on any long-term goal, the short-term steps — at least the first ones — become obvious, for every long-term goal consists of a series of short-term goals. Mark Twain put it so simply and clearly:

> *"The secret of getting ahead is getting started. The secret of getting started is breaking your complex, overwhelming tasks into small manageable tasks, and then starting on the first one.*

"When I set up my long-range goal of creating a successful business, I had no idea of all the short-term steps necessary to reach that goal. But the first short-term goals seemed obvious: Get a job, save some money, then use that money to finance my next step, whatever that may turn out to be. Once I reached those goals, the next series of short-term goals became obvious. By keeping the long-range goal of a *successful* company in mind, I was led to discover how to create a successful business, step by step.

"The goal I wrote wasn't just, *I have a successful company.* It was more specific and measurable: *I have a business with an income of over x dollars a year and pre-tax profits of over twenty percent of that income.*

"I made that same goal, for many years, with larger numbers for the year ahead. It's fun to make goals that specific — and even more fun to reach them.

"When I look back on my first short-term goals, it's kind of amusing to me now to see how *small* my thinking was. Because my thinking was small, my company remained small. It continued to remain small until I was able to increase the scope of my vision. The size of my business reflected — and continues to reflect — the size of my thinking. The more I grow, the more I can stretch to create higher goals, the more my business prospers.

"Every long-term goal can be broken down into a series of short-term goals. Developing these goals is an ever-changing, ongoing process. It involves playing with every possibility that comes to mind, then sitting down and making a list of priorities."

**The Fourth Key:
Create short-term goals
that move you toward
your long-term goals.**

"Short-term goals are the goals you put into your daily calendar, whatever you carry with you for appointments and to remind you to do things on a daily or weekly basis. Sit with each one of your long-term goals, reflect on it, and then put the short-term goals that come to mind into your calendar.

"Once you've got your notebook or calendar and you're using it almost every day, the elements of your power kit, or magician's tool kit — or whatever you want to call it — are all in place: You have your folder with your long-term goals and other things we've discussed, and you have your calendar to keep you organized and assist you in reaching your short-term goals easily and effortlessly.

"Think of your notebook or calendar as the conduit between your long-term goals and your daily life. Whatever form of calendar you have, it should be something that allows you to take those long-range goals you're affirming to yourself and break them down into short-term steps you can clearly map out."

Bernie settled back into his chair and closed his eyes for a long moment. When he finally spoke, his voice was quiet, yet more forceful, and his eyes remained half-closed.

THE MYSTERY OF CREATION

"I've seen, repeatedly, that this system of creating long-term goals and breaking them down into short-term goals works. But I've often wondered *how* it works. The answer, it seems to me, involves a mystery — the mystery of creation — and so it's subtle and difficult to understand. Maybe it's impossible to fully understand. Yet it's worth reflecting on — and it's something I find fascinating.

"The way I see it, *a subtle but powerfully creative process is set in motion when a long-range goal is supported by focused short-term activities.*

"On the surface, it seems obvious: We create long-term goals on paper, repeat them so we'll remember them, and then break them down into short-term goals. Of course this helps us achieve our goals.

"But it's not as simple as it seems, for if it were, a great many more people would be doing it, and being successful. To actually do it requires a certain amount of intelligence and discipline — enough intelligence to grasp the concept, and enough discipline to review your long-term goals regularly and to work with your calendar nearly every day to stay focused on your short-term goals.

"Once you start this process, and focus firmly and clearly

on your goals, you'll discover you've begun to release, or connect with, a mysterious energy. The first indications of it
working are usually the number of 'coincidences' that start
happening that move you toward your goal in ways you
couldn't have foreseen. Simply by creating a goal and making
a step toward it, you've set in motion powerful creative
forces. I've seen this happen over and over.

"The reason is mysterious but very real: *As soon as you
commit yourself to a goal that's in alignment with your purpose
in life, and as soon as you take even one concrete step toward
that goal, you have created or connected with an energy that
has an impact upon the world, and causes other things to happen, externally, beyond your conscious control, that assist you
in moving toward that goal.*

"We're evolving beings, and by moving forward, consciously, in our evolution, we subconsciously summon the
power of nature, the power of the universe, to assist us. It's
not necessary to know *why* this miracle works. All we need to
know is that by daring to stretch out and reach for our highest dreams, aspirations, and mission in life, we'll receive the
support we need.

"The great German writer Goethe summed it up beautifully in two famous lines of poetry:

"*Whatever you can do, or dream you can, begin it.
Boldness has genius, power, and magic in it.*

"Genius, power, and magic! All three come from sources
beyond our conscious mind. And all three are summoned by

imagining our highest goals and taking that first small step, even if it seems tentative, scary, or childish.

"Even small steps are powerful. Once you put several of them together, you've taken a giant step.

"And small steps are powerful because they affirm to our limitless, ingenious subconscious mind that we've created a goal of where we want to go in life, and we've infused ourselves with power by being willing to take whatever action is necessary to move ourselves toward that goal."

Bernie sat motionless; his eyes were fully closed now. He stayed that way for quite a while. I relaxed and closed my eyes, as well. It felt like such a good thing to do, and yet was something I so rarely did.

We sat calmly, quietly, hearing the distant, muffled sounds of the activity in the lobby below.

KEY FIVE:

Visualize Your Success

There is nothing at all new, strange, or unusual about creative visualization. You are already using it every day, every minute in fact.

— Shakti Gawain, *Creative Visualization*

I splurged and bought a beautiful weekly calendar that had nature photos on every left-hand page. I took all the long-term goals from my folder and tried to enter the first short-term steps into my calendar. I had no difficulty knowing what those steps were for my business, but stalled on how to own a home, and how to create a long-term relationship. How do you come up with short-term goals for those?

Starting to save for a down payment on a house would certainly be a good way to begin; so would learning a little more about real estate. I wrote *Create an account for a down payment* in my calendar on the day after I would receive my next paycheck, and I added *Read real estate info in Sunday's paper* into my calendar.

I was clueless about starting a new relationship, though — which was obviously why I didn't have one. Maybe just opening up to the possibility of having one would be enough, though that seemed far too vague for a goal — certainly something I couldn't enter in my calendar anywhere. Maybe setting aside some time for socializing and maybe even for reflection about a relationship would be a good start.

When I thought about it, I had a great deal of guilt around my relationships. I had been close to a few women, over the years, but always felt I needed to get my life together first, at least financially, before I was ready for a committed relationship or a family.

I thought Bernie would probably have some insight into this enigmatic area of life. It seemed, at least from a distance, he had a peaceful and satisfying family life.

A week or so passed before Bernie came strolling into my office again. It was early evening; everyone else had gone home for the day. I was trying to fulfill one of the short-term goals I had put in my calendar several days before: updating our projections of income for the next year.

He arrived just in time to hear me let out an audible groan of frustration.

"Are we having fun yet?" he said.

"Oh...not really," I said. "I'm trying to do our projections for the next twelve months. It's frustrating."

He looked at me calmly, nodded and smiled.

"If I try to be realistic," I said, "I feel like we're going nowhere at all. If I try to be optimistic, it feels like I'm making projections we'll never achieve."

Bernie sat down in a chair in front of my desk and looked at me again, almost quizzically, as if he had a question for me, or was assessing something. But he didn't say a word. The pause felt uncomfortable.

"Can I get you something?" I said.

"No, I'm fine." And there was another moment of awkward silence. Then he nodded his head.

"Do you have time for the next key?" he said.

"Sure."

"Maybe there's something in this next step you'll find useful, or inspiring, or whatever."

I found the tape recorder, and Bernie launched right into it, as soon as I clicked it on.

"Okay, you've already created, mentally and on paper, a clear picture of what you want in life — your ideal scene — and you've begun to take the first steps in that direction. Now you're ready for the next step. It's more than a step, it's an ongoing process. A tremendous key to success.

"I've known so many people over the years who have had wonderful dreams, and have taken some steps to achieve them, yet their dreams elude them, over and over. What keeps going wrong? Usually, one — or more — of these things:

"One, they're not effectively visualizing their success. It's never become a subconscious *intention*.

"Two, they're letting their doubts and fears overwhelm them. Doubt and fear are stronger than their vision.

"Three, they aren't doing what's in alignment with their purpose or mission in life.

"The first two reasons are *inextricably* linked." He nearly spit the word at me. "Once you let your visualization fade, doubts and fears overwhelm you. If your doubts and fears are stronger than your dreams, you'll fail to create those dreams.

"Our doubts, fears, and dreams all have one thing in common: they take place within us, in our own mind. *All our problems, and all our successes, are creations of our own mind.*"

Bernie's eyes were wide open, bright and clear. He spoke rapidly and forcefully.

OUR INTERNAL GAUGE

"Someone asked me a very good question once, years ago: *What was the single most difficult thing you had to deal with in achieving success?* I said, immediately, *My own mind.* That's where all the work is, in my mind. And a visual image sprang to mind, something I've never forgotten:

"We all have an internal gauge of some sort in our mind — at least symbolically. The way I imagine it, it looks almost like a gas gauge, with a needle that swings from left to right, like this . . ."

He took a pen from his pocket and pulled an old envelope out of my waste basket and made a crude drawing:

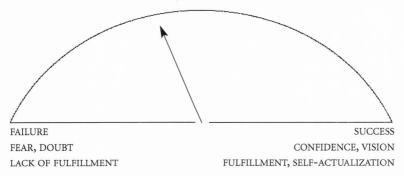

FAILURE   SUCCESS
FEAR, DOUBT   CONFIDENCE, VISION
LACK OF FULFILLMENT   FULFILLMENT, SELF-ACTUALIZATION

"The gauge fluctuates with every thought; the needle
swings from one end to the other instantly, in the time it
takes to have *one thought*. One end of the gauge is doubt,
cynicism, fear, confusion. The eternal pessimist. The other
end of the gauge is confidence, hope, belief, love. Our highest
dreams, wishes, visions, goals. The eternal visionary; the creative genius.

"As long as my needle is *predominantly* on the side of
doubt and fear, nothing happens, and success remains an elusive goal. I visualize, and therefore create, nothing but failure.
But every dream, goal, vision, and confident thought I have
swings the needle over to the other side, *immediately*. When I
focus on my ideal scene, I swing to that side in an instant.

"As soon as my needle averages somewhere near the middle, magic starts to happen. My hopes and dreams start
becoming realities.

"The main work, the most effective work I've done, has
been within my mind — holding more and more of the

vision of my dreams and my ideal scene in my mind. Then I take steps toward those dreams, and that reinforces my confidence, hope, and belief.

"James Allen summed it up in *As You Think:*

> *"You will become as great as your dominant aspiration.... If you cherish a vision, a lofty ideal in your heart, You will realize it."*

He said the words forcefully, from memory, with great emphasis on each word. It felt like he was trying to imprint them indelibly into my brain. I had never seen Bernie so animated. He seemed like a different person — the manic brother of the laid-back guy with the half-closed eyes I had seen last time.

"This is why *affirmations* are so powerful, so effective. An affirmation is just a positive thought, and it moves us to the right side of our internal gauge. A single affirmation can move us from fear and doubt to *attainment.*

"The image of this gauge kept coming to mind, and I reflected on it quite a bit. It was a new way to measure the quality of my thoughts, whether I was visualizing for good or ill, success or failure. I kept noticing, over and over, where my thoughts were on the gauge. If my thoughts were fearful, envious, jealous, or angry, I tried to find out how to move into acceptance, forgiveness, love, creative possibilities, goals, visions, dreams... how to let go of resentment... how to find the opportunities within the problems. Thoughts of success rather than failure. Visionary thoughts, that help you remember and rekindle your dreams."

THE SEVEN LEVELS OF CONSCIOUSNESS

"The more I thought about the image of that internal gauge, the more details came to be added. I realized it encompasses all the different levels of our consciousness. Years ago I read a book called *The Handbook to Higher Consciousness,* by Ken Keyes, Jr. It was a breakthrough book for me, a brilliant blend of Eastern and Western psychology, revolving around our levels of consciousness — called *chakras* in the East — that correspond to our physical, emotional, mental, and spiritual levels of being."

As he said *physical* he put his hands solidly on his thighs. As he said *emotional* he put his left hand on his stomach, and his right hand on his heart. As he said *mental* he framed his head with his hands. As he said *spiritual,* he looked up and held his arms out.

"One reason we're here in life is to experience *all* these levels of consciousness, and to master the teachings each one has for us."

He drew another diagram on the envelope as he spoke.

"Our first level of consciousness is too often dominated by *fear;* the second by *jealousy and envy;* the third by *anger.* Yet each level of consciousness has a vitally important reason for being — each one is a center of power that needs to be explored and eventually mastered.

"Our first level is called our *root chakra.*" He put his hands solidly on his thighs again.

"It's our base level, our grounding in physical reality, our roots in the earth, our ancestry. It's also the seat of our fears, and we need to learn that within our fear is a great gift. Our fear is a brilliant intuitive feedback system that helps us protect ourselves in the world. There is a very good reason for our fear. But in most of us, our fears are exaggerated and unreasonable. We fear far too much; our fears are unfounded.

"Instead of fear and insecurity, the challenge is to find complete acceptance and security, even *serenity,* in this level of consciousness, this center of power, for it's here we find our connection with our Mother Earth, and Mother Earth provides for us, abundantly, if we believe it's so. If we believe we live in an abundant world, in an abundant universe, that belief becomes self-fulfilling. If we believe there's not enough to go around — what we call *scarcity programming* — then that becomes true in our experience.

"Each level of consciousness contains its own path to enlightenment, to freedom, success, whatever we want to call it. Each one has a question to ponder, a *koan,* as they call it in Zen Buddhism. Reflecting on the *koan,* and ultimately understanding it, is a key to mastering that particular path.

"Questions for the first center of consciousness are:

> *"What is the gift of my fear?*
> *"How can I find security in the midst of my fear?*
> *"How can I turn my fear into serenity?"*

He sat for a moment in silence. His voice had grown quiet, yet he was still fervent.

"The second level of consciousness centers around our generative organs, our sexuality" — he opened his hands on his lap — "the force of the creation of new life, and the source of tremendous physical and creative energy. It's where our jealousy and envy are centered, as well, but we don't need to be overwhelmed by jealousy and envy when we're in this center of consciousness and power — the challenge is to find out how to *glory* in our creative fulfillment, how to be joyous, free, grateful for all the gifts we've been given.

"The *koan,* the question to ponder for the second center, is:

> *"How can I turn my jealousy into fulfillment, into self-actualization?*
> *"How can I find joyous freedom and fulfillment within my jealousy and envy?"*

We thought about that for a while.

"The third level of our consciousness is centered right here" — he placed both hands solidly on his stomach — "the Japanese call it *hara,* and understand it better than we do. It's the source of our *power:* physical power to impact our world. It's also the seat of our anger, and the challenge is to find out how to go beyond anger, into the joy and satisfaction of fully expressing our power, being ever more capable and successful in the world, in any way we desire.

"The question to ponder for the third center is:

> *"How can I turn my anger into power — power*
> *to fulfill my greatest dreams?"*

We sat in silence again. Bernie's back was straight. He looked much more imposing, suddenly, as if he had physically grown bigger.

Then he raised both hands to his heart, and took a deep breath.

"The fourth level of consciousness is centered in our hearts: it's *love,* of course, and love can overcome all the problems associated with the first three centers. Love is the answer; love is the key. It's the answer to the question of how to deal with our fear, envy, and anger. It's the key that opens the doors to the higher centers of creative expression, vision, and ultimate understanding and wisdom." He gestured to his throat, forehead, and beyond.

"The *koan* for this center is simply:

> *"How can I remember to stay in my heart?*
> *"How can I always remember the healing power*
> *of love?"*

I breathed deeply into my chest as we sat in silence. Then Bernie held both hands in front of his throat and jaw.

"Beyond love is creative expression; once we do what we love, we naturally become creative, and want to share it with others. It's centered in our throats; it's where we give voice to what's in our hearts and minds.

"This is the fifth center of power, and the *koan* is:

"How can I fulfill my creative expression?
"How can I fulfill my potential?"

He looked at me almost as if he expected an answer. Then he smiled and closed his eyes and touched his forehead.

"Beyond that, and closely connected to it, is our inner, visionary level of consciousness and power, centered between our eyebrows — our 'third eye', the source of our inner vision. It's where your consciousness is when you imagine your ideal scene. Every great artist, every visionary, every spiritual leader understands this level of consciousness. So does every truly successful person, in their own way. It's where we focus the power of our minds.

"The question to ponder for this center is:

"How can I see my inner vision?
"What are my greatest dreams?"

He sat absolutely still, eyes closed, hands relaxed in his lap, for a long moment. I closed my eyes as well.

"Keep your eyes closed as I describe the next one," Bernie said.

"Beyond that plane of vision is the highest level, the seventh: union with the universe, with God, in whatever words you use to describe the forces of creation. We are one with the quantum field, the nonlocal mind — whatever you want to call it. In this level of consciousness, we realize the truth that mystics and physicists know: Everything we perceive as form is emptiness; we are part of one great field of energy and information, one vast interconnected ocean of atoms. We are part of one great whole, infused with a great spirit.

"The *koan* for this is:

> *"How can I experience the truth... the reality of the universe... union with all that is?*

"Find your own words, whatever resonates for you."

We sat in silence for a long time. Then Bernie nearly whispered, "A yoga teacher in India put it this way:

> *"Close your eyes, and see God.*

"In any way you define or understand God. This is the center of prayer, creation, and grace."

More silence. God looked like an endless ocean of light.

Bernie finally took a deep, noisy breath and came out of his meditation. He wrote a few more words on the envelope and drew an arc, completing a new chart:

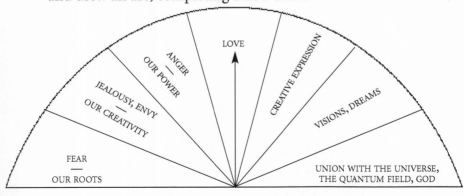

OUR CENTERS OF CONSCIOUSNESS AND POWER

"Is this getting too esoteric for you?" he asked with a grin.

"No, not at all." The so-called esoteric had always intrigued me, especially since it seemed that scientists as well as mystics had gotten pretty esoteric in the last half of the twentieth century.

"Good — it's worthwhile to reflect on things like this, at least for me. It's not for everybody, but some people find it inspiring — some have found it *enlightening*. But now I'll get more concrete:

"This chart shows why *the key to success in life is doing what we love to do*. Even if we have all kinds of fearful thoughts when we think of changing, growing, improving our lives in some way; even if we have ingrained beliefs that *it's so hard to succeed;* even if we're envious, jealous, or angry a lot of the time; if we keep on doing what we love to do, we automatically get to a higher level of consciousness — our heart center — and in that moment we overcome our fears and doubts, envy and anger.

"When we do what we love, we get good at it, skilled, creative. When our creativity develops, we start to see how it can lead us to our success — and so our vision becomes clearer. Once we have a vision of success that we support with our creativity, love, and power, *nothing* can stop us.

"And ultimately, by doing what we love, by expressing our creativity, and by connecting with our vision, we overcome our fear of failure, fear of success, fear of every kind, envy of others, and anger.

"All the important work we need to do is within us,

within our minds and bodies. Once we have done the work within us, the whole world magically showers us with success.

"Do you understand what I mean?"

All I could do was nod. Bernie stared at me for a moment before he went on.

"The most powerful work we can do is *visualizing*. When we visualize our ideal scene, when we imagine our success, we're automatically exalted to a higher level of consciousness — the needle instantly shifts to the side of fulfillment — and it's from that side that we connect with the forces of creation.

"This step is vital — without it, nothing can be achieved."

The Fifth Key:
Visualize your success, and keep
the visualization strong by renewing it often.

"It's *essential* to take the time to consciously visualize your success. Take your list of long-term goals, and focus on each one of them individually. Imagine yourself attaining those goals, and keep the visualization strong by renewing it often.

"With nearly every goal you create — for reasons we'll get into in the next step — you'll probably have doubts and fears, mental and emotional resistance. These doubts and fears combine to form powerful negative images that can only be overcome through powerful positive visualization.

"You'll never succeed in anything if your fears and doubts outweigh your belief in your ability to succeed. *You will become as great as your dominant aspiration,* as James Allen put it. If your dominant aspiration is clouded with fear and doubt, you'll realize those fears and doubts instead of success, because you haven't seen your success clearly.

"You create whatever you dwell on and visualize consistently — no more, no less.

"As you focus on each one of your goals, *feel* yourself attaining it. Create a picture of it in your mind — see it, as clearly as you can, and feel it as well. Keep on holding it in your mind and heart. Eventually, your visualization becomes so clear that one day you find you can step right into it, in *reality,* and discover — in a wonderful rush of realization — that you've created exactly what you've been dreaming of all along.

"Eventually, your life will change so dramatically that every time you look around at the home and work environments you've created, you'll visualize success, for you'll see it right before your eyes."

I've often imagined that when Jesus spoke, and Buddha spoke, their words rang with the clarity of truth. No one who heard their words with an open mind and heart could doubt the obvious truth in what they said.

It was the same with Bernie that day. He looked at me with clear, shining eyes, and he spoke the undeniable truth.

Hearing it and practicing it, however, were two very different things. When I looked around my musty little office, when I thought of my dusty little apartment, I knew I had a lot to learn about effective visualization.

Learn to Face Your Emotions, and See the Gift in Each One

The fact that you are the maker of your character, the molder of your life, and the builder of your destiny, you may unerringly prove, if you will watch, control, and alter your thoughts, tracing their effects upon yourself, upon others, and upon your life and circumstances . . . and utilizing your every experience as a means of obtaining that knowledge of yourself that leads to understanding, wisdom, and power.

— James Allen, *As You Think*

T he week that followed was probably the most difficult week of my life. Monday morning began with a major crisis: The company that was our sole distributor suddenly closed its doors and went into bankruptcy, with no advance warning. Most of our inventory was locked up in their warehouse, and we couldn't even get to it. It may or may not have been seized by banks or other creditors. There were lawyers, threats, people blaming other people, upset bankers, charges of mismanagement, even charges of fraud. We had been caught unaware and unprepared. The whole mess was so complex I couldn't even understand its endless convoluted details. And all the key players involved seemed to have a totally different version of what went on and who was to blame (never themselves). I felt naive and stupid. Hurt and angry and overwhelmed. Maybe I was in the wrong business. Why was it such a struggle?

It certainly was not happening in an easy and relaxed manner, in a healthy and positive way. We all worked from early morning into the night, until we were exhausted, just trying to survive the crisis and keep from going bankrupt ourselves.

I didn't give one thought to Bernie's words all week. I ran furiously and got nowhere — or worse, deeper and deeper into trouble. By Friday, I was a basket case. And so was everyone else in the company.

Bernie came strolling in nonchalantly, as always, just as some tempers flared in the front office. Everyone in the company, all six of us, were there. It was not a pretty sight. At the sight of Bernie, though, we all cooled down — or at least shut up.

He just smiled as if he thought it all very amusing.

"I have an off-the-wall idea for you," he said to everyone. "It's...let's see...almost four. What if I came back in an hour or so, and gave a little talk? Any of you who are interested can listen."

Four of us were interested. Two had other plans.

He came back later with a cappuccino in hand, and we sat in a motley assortment of chairs in a circle in the front area. We gave Bernie the special chair; it was funky, like all the rest, but it had nice arms on it. He sat as if he were on a throne.

He started by telling the others about the book project, and said he felt maybe they'd all benefit by hearing the next step or two. I got out the trusty tape recorder. Bernie sat comfortably and spoke quietly.

"Here's what we've done up to now: We've explored the first important keys to changing our lives and world for the better. We've learned that we're all visionaries, we're all magicians, though most of us use our magical powers to barely create enough to pay the rent, rather than creating what we want in life. So we've taken steps to remedy this: We've created an ideal scene, one that's aligned with our greatest purpose or mission in life. Starting with our ideal scene, we've created a clear mental map of where we want to go in life, and we've started moving step by step, goal by goal, toward it. We're visualizing our success, and keeping the visualization fresh in our mind.

"Most of these keys have involved *mental* processes — focusing our thoughts. Now we're ready for another key, the key to *creating what we want emotionally.*

"Now, that phrase has two meanings: we need to put emotional energy into the things we want to create, *and* we need to learn how to create the kind of life we want emotionally, as well. We can learn how to move past fear, envy, jealousy, and anger. These things can be taught; they can be learned. We can learn how to have a much more satisfying emotional experience much more of the time.

"We grow emotionally, just as we grow physically and mentally. As we grow emotionally, our life experience gets much more fun. We enjoy life a lot more. We become wiser, more fulfilled. We even become, much of the time, happy, grateful, calm, and clear. Even *serene.*"

He said the word slowly, with serenity.

"The key to experiencing these states more often is in learning how to deal effectively with all our so-called negative emotions, and beliefs, and problems that prevent us from getting what we want in life *in an easy and relaxed manner, in a healthy and positive way.*

"It's not only possible, it's *desirable* to create a life experience for ourselves that's emotionally satisfying. We don't *need* to be under constant stress at work, or frustrated at home. We don't *need* to be adversely affected by our frenetic, workaholic society. We don't *need* to be trapped in addictive behavior. We don't *need* to feel pressured about money, or resentful about past or present relationships. It's much more satisfying to be happy, content, to enjoy life. These are worthwhile goals — and there are tools you can use to achieve these goals.

"Creating a life that's satisfying emotionally doesn't mean we deny in any way, or repress, so-called negative emotions. *Every one* of our emotions is valuable, important, and necessary, and none are to be denied. Every one gives us vast amounts of intuitive knowledge, when we tune into it. But it's certainly valuable to create a vision of a life that's emotionally satisfying, and to take steps toward realizing that vision.

"To create the kind of life we want, the life we envision in our ideal scene, we need to repeatedly focus on our emotional states, and on our deepest-held beliefs that fuel those emotional states, and make sure we're not sabotaging ourselves from achieving our dreams.

"We can easily *imagine* the kind of life we want. It's fun to picture an ideal scene; it's fun to create goals and affirm that we're reaching them in an easy and relaxed manner, in a healthy and positive way.

"As soon as we create any worthwhile goal, though, we're challenging ourselves to expand, to *evolve,* to explore new territory. As soon as we do that, we encounter our own emotional resistance, and we reach what is for many people the most important key to fulfillment."

The Sixth Key:
Learn to face your emotions,
and see the gift in each one.

"This isn't rocket science. There are pretty simple techniques you can learn that can change your emotional reactions to life's trials and hardships and challenges. Once you do the techniques, you begin to understand the principles behind them, and see that they're true *because the techniques work.*"

Bernie sat quiet and motionless for a long beat. He had been talking softly, and we were listening carefully. It was relaxing... vaguely hypnotic in some way.

"Before we can create what we want in life, we have to deal effectively with our emotional resistance. This is important to understand. It has to become an ongoing awareness — *knowledge* that we apply constantly in our daily lives. As we explore our emotional resistance in depth, we take our knowledge to heart, and it becomes wisdom — an understanding of our emotions that can change our lives and, ultimately, bring us happiness. *Fulfillment.*"

EMOTIONAL RESISTANCE

"We've created goals that feel wonderful, goals that are aligned with our highest purpose in life, goals that expand us and move us much closer to our dreams of happiness and fulfillment. We're affirming to ourselves regularly that we're achieving these goals in an easy and relaxed manner, in a healthy and positive way.

"Yet with so many of these goals, we encounter emotional resistance, in so many different forms: endless varieties of fear, skepticism, doubt, anxiety, disbelief, self-criticism, excuses, procrastination, self-defeating habits. We have inner voices that tell us *we don't deserve to be successful,* for some reason — we don't have the ability, the talent, the connections, the money, the time, the education, the luck, or whatever it takes to create what we want in life.

"Why do we have this emotional resistance in the first place? Why do we resist our own success? Within the answer to this question is the knowledge, and ultimately the wisdom, that helps us overcome our emotional resistance.

"Ask yourself this question, and try to answer as honestly as possible: *Why do I resist creating what I want in life?*"

He paused and looked around at each of us, giving us plenty of time to think about his question. No easy answer came to mind. I knew I had fears, fears of... what? Fear of failure. Fear of bankruptcy. Fear of criticism. Fear of hurting people in some way. And it seems so difficult to create what I want, so hard to succeed! It's a huge challenge, with so much hard work involved. I didn't know if I had what it takes. Those were my fears, at that moment.

"It's not a simple question, I know," Bernie said. "Look at the following possibilities, and see if one or more of them describes your experience:

"As soon as we create a worthwhile goal, we're challenging ourselves to expand, to explore new territory — and *new territory can be frightening.* We're forcing ourselves to be creative, we've begun our *conscious evolution,* and it means growing and changing and doing new things in new ways. This brings up a lot of emotional resistance in most people.

"And every goal involves taking a risk, and *taking risks is frightening.* Every risk we take, after all, has the possibility of failure — and almost all of us fear failure. Failure can mean poverty; it can mean loss of self-respect and self-esteem; it can mean ridicule, or pity, from people we respect; it can mean our worst fears are realized. And what are our worst fears? Death? Destitution? Creating a hell on earth? *All our fears are unfounded.*"

He said that with quiet passion. Then he smiled broadly.

"As it says in the old gospel hymn: *O Mary, don't you weep, don't you moan, all your fears are unfounded, O Mary, don't you weep.*"

He laughed at himself. "I'm getting off track here. We were talking about reasons for resisting success:

"Success means making goals, trying to create something that's not happening now. Making new goals means changing in some way, and this upsets our old, comfortable habits. The power of old habits can be a strong force that works against us when we try to change for the better. Even if we're extremely frustrated with our current situation, at least it's familiar to us, and we're comfortable with it, at least subconsciously. As Hamlet said, we would rather bear those ills we have, than fly to others we know not of.

"Many people fear success itself. We're at least subconsciously aware that success will bring with it lots of new and challenging problems. We might have the belief that success would bring too much stress to handle, or too much work, too many responsibilities that would take all the fun out of life. And the more successful we are, the more we're criticized by others. A safe way to avoid criticism is not to succeed too brilliantly.

"Or we might even fear that success will cost us too much — maybe, like Faust, it'll cost us our souls.

"New goals, based on our dreams and ideals, directly confront — and contradict — a vast amount of negative conditioning we've learned over the course of our lives, all of the deep limiting beliefs we've heard and accepted as our own.

"There's a great book, *Embracing Our Selves,* by Hal and Sidra Stone, that shows us how multifaceted we are, how each of us has a great number of subpersonalities, and they're are often in conflict with each other. Each of us has a creative child still within us, and a vulnerable child, and an inner critic. We have a 'pusher', driving us to do more and more, a 'protector/controller' trying to maintain order and the status quo, and a great many other subpersonalities. Some are dominant, while others are disowned.

"Each subpersonality has a great number of beliefs about itself — some positive, some negative. Each of us senses on some level, for instance, that we really are creative and unique and have something important to contribute to the world — *but* we may also have come to believe that we're really not that creative, we can't make much difference in the world, and it's hardly worth the risk and effort to try to fulfill our unrealistic dreams. They're just insubstantial fantasies, aren't they? Aren't we getting too big for our britches?

"We all have a creative child within us — a creative genius, actually — but too often it's outshouted, overshadowed by a cynical inner critic who has seen it all and knows it can be done better than you can do it, and it doesn't make any difference anyway, so why bother? The inner critic is very vocal in most of us. It's intelligent, agile, adept, and *never* happy with what we're doing. We have to learn when to ignore it, and let our creative genius be free to take risks and make mistakes.

"We pick up a great deal of negative conditioning over the course of our lives, and a lot of deep beliefs, *core* beliefs, that limit us and prevent us from creating what we want. It's not easy for most of us to confront and deal effectively with these deep-seated beliefs.

"Years ago, I went through a process that does just that. It was written in *The Creative Visualization Workbook* by Shakti Gawain. It should be better known, and practiced widely. This information is worth repeating, until it becomes common knowledge. Doing this exercise leads to wisdom."

He was still speaking quietly. And he emphasized certain words strangely, drawing them out slowly rather than saying them louder, as most people do. The quieter he spoke, the more intensely he spoke. I'd never quite heard anything like it.

AN OPEN ATTITUDE

"It's not necessary to *believe* that any of these ideas or exercises will work for you. You only have to dare to try something new, and experiment a bit. Try the exercise that follows — *the core belief process* — with an open mind, and see what happens. Don't accept what I say or what anyone else says as truth, until you have tested it in the laboratory of your own experience. Then form your own conclusions. The information you get from others has to become your own knowledge.

"These ideas and techniques have worked for me, and they'll work for anyone who applies them consistently in their life. All that's needed is an open mind. Open yourself up to the possibility that you and your world can be totally different from what you believe at the moment. There are many, many people who believe differently than you do, who believe it's possible to succeed *brilliantly* at whatever they dream of. They're the ones who succeed. So go ahead! Entertain different possibilities! Open up to the *idea* of change. It may be frightening at times, but it's time for a change, individually and globally. Look at it as an adventure, a great experiment — one that can improve your life, and the world as well.

"I *strongly* encourage you to do the following exercise, and go through the steps of the core belief process — more than once. Question and challenge the material, and question and challenge yourself. It's time well spent."

He smiled. "Better than watching TV," he said.

CLEARING PSYCHOLOGICAL BLOCKS

"All of us have some psychological blocks that affect our

attitudes and behavior in some ways. These blocks are built on various fears we've developed during our lives — usually quite early in life. They're obstacles that prevent us from realizing our greatest potential, because they prevent us from taking risks, trying new things, making positive changes.

"Doubts, worries, and fears inhibit us. They create low self-esteem and an overly critical attitude toward ourselves, and others as well. Much of what we consider 'normal' behavior really stems from fear: Worried parents, frustrated kids, and highly stressful work environments are often accepted as 'normal', or even inevitable, yet these situations can be changed. No universal law says that parents have to worry, kids have to be frustrated, and work environments have to be stressful.

"These emotional states can be changed — the challenge is to take an honest look at them, and discover how to move beyond them. The process isn't difficult, but it does require willingness to change, to let go of old, familiar habit patterns.

"If you haven't created the kind of life you want, if you haven't attained the kind of success you dream of, you can be sure you have some psychological blocks to examine, and to let go of. It can be done. Many others have done it, and more are doing it every day."

ACCEPTANCE

"The first step in this process is overlooked sometimes, but it's important. The first step is *to completely accept your-*

self, as you are, right now. If you can fully accept yourself, you'll find it much easier to change for the better. *It's all right to have negative feelings,* and you have a lot of company if you do — the entire human race, in fact.

"Actually, so-called negative feelings are beneficial in many ways — each one has its own gift for us. They keep us discontent, for one thing, so we're forced to examine ourselves. And that's necessary to grow and develop, and eventually become stronger, clearer, wiser — able to fulfill our potential in life.

"I was neurotic in a lot of ways when I was young. My 'normal' state of mind was full of anxiety. I was afraid of death, afraid of the future, afraid of failure. I resented people. I resented my father, the educational system, conservatives, bigots — the list goes on and on. Now I'm glad I was neurotic — my resentment forced me to look at myself, and to question everything.

"Neuroses can be good for you, because they force you to examine your life. They force you to do things that make you grow — read some books, or go to a therapist or seminar of some kind, or a twelve-step meeting, or a church or Zen center, or to the East, or the desert, or the mountains.

"My frustration and resentment forced me to drop out of the rat race and search for something else. It led to learning everything I'm telling you. It led me to discover I could create exactly what I wanted in life, nothing more, nothing less.

"And the first step is *to accept* exactly where you are, in this moment. Ask yourself if there are things you don't accept about yourself, things you're frustrated, guilty, angry, or fearful about. Take an honest look at all of your feelings, one at a time, and embrace each one as being, for the present, a perfectly acceptable part of you. *Embrace all your selves,* every part of your being. All these things have been necessary for your development so far. All have things to teach you, gifts for you. Accept them, and you'll find it much easier to either live with them or let them go — whatever happens.

"Accept your friends and family, as they are, as well. Accept your boss and co-workers. Accept everyone you come in contact with, even those you dislike or disagree with. Accept everyone on the planet. We're all doing the best we can. Some are trying to hold the old forms together, some are trying to create new ones. Some are failing, some succeeding. Each of us is making our unique contribution to the tapestry of life.

"Acceptance doesn't mean you have to put up with anything you don't feel good about, or you can't express your honest feelings to others. Quite the contrary — once you really accept yourself and others, you find it much easier to give honest feedback, and this feedback is more effective, more readily heard. We'll deal with that in the next step — the next key. For now, we're dealing with our emotions."

CORE BELIEFS

"Why do we resist change, and success? What's at the root of it all? Once we find the cause, we've taken a giant step toward the cure.

"A great many psychologists, teachers, therapists, scientists, religious people, philosophers, intellectuals, writers, neurotics, psychotics, and others have tried to answer these questions with a great many theories, including heredity, environment, our parents, our dysfunctional family, genetic coding, disease, cultural heritage, co-dependence, physical defects, mental defects, misplaced sexual energy, disowned selves, emotional instability, lack of roots, sins we've committed, evil in the world, our lack of understanding, ignorance of the laws of karma, and *lots* of other reasons that a great many creative, sometimes desperate, imaginations have devised."

Bernie had to stop and chuckle. His eyes were heavy lidded. He looked to be in some kind of amused reverie.

"Most of these theories blame things beyond our control, and that makes it difficult, if not impossible, to change our behavior. How can we change our early environment — now a thing of the past — or a dysfunctional family? And it's certainly impossible to change our heredity, genetic coding, or parents.

"We have to not only find the causes of our resistance and blocks, *we need to understand these causes in a way that enables us to do something about them.* Now consider the following theory. Live with it and work with it awhile, and see if you find it useful: *The causes of our psychological blocks are the particular 'core beliefs' we have formed about ourselves, other people, and our world.* A 'core belief' is an idea or attitude we *accept as truth,* consciously or unconsciously — whether it's true or not.

"This can be a powerful concept, worth exploring. For once we understand it and work with it, we discover the power to change our lives for the better.

"In earliest childhood, we learn to accept certain things as either true or false in our world. Many of these things were oft-repeated words from Mommy or Daddy: We're good little kids, or bad kids, bright or stupid, or sloppy, or silly, or pretty, or goofy-looking, or dirty, or talented, or lazy, or hyperactive, or moody, or withdrawn . . . the list goes on and on. Many of these ideas were things our brothers, sisters, and peers told us, and we accepted them, unconsciously.

"Our experience in the school system usually adds a great many negative, limiting core beliefs as well, with grading systems, highly competitive sports, pressure for popularity, IQ tests, and other assorted garbage. From a very early age, we develop some deep feelings of *inadequacy*. Very few students come out of the school system with a positive self-image, daring to dream of the greatest success imaginable. Very few students leave school feeling like a winner — and yet we can *all* become winners, each in our own way, once we understand the power of our core beliefs.

"Many of these beliefs are harmful and negative; some are contradictory, and cause confusion; some are positive and supportive. Here are some typical negative, limiting core beliefs."

He took a deep breath and spoke quietly and dramatically, saying each with a smile:

"I'm inadequate; I'm not complete in some way; I need someone else or something else to be happy; I'm incapable; it's so hard to succeed; so few people succeed; money doesn't grow

on trees; it's impossible to make enough money these days; I don't know how to manage money — if I had it, I'd probably just blow it anyway; the world is a dangerous place; it's a jungle out there; life is a struggle, and you always lose in the end; my parents didn't raise me right; I had a deprived childhood; deep down, I can't really love anyone; love is dangerous — I might get hurt, or hurt someone; I don't really have any close friends; I'm not okay; there's something wrong with me; I'm unworthy and undeserving; people (including me) are basically bad — selfish, cruel, stupid, untrustworthy, sinful; there's not enough love (or money, or good things) to go around, so I have to struggle to get my share; there's not enough time — I never have enough time to do what I need to do; being successful would mean eighty-hour work weeks or other things I'm not willing to do, or able to do; it's hopeless, I'll never get enough; if I have a lot, someone else will have to do without; if I get rich, I'll lose my soul; money is the root of all evil; money corrupts; the rich get richer and the poor get poorer; the world doesn't work and never will — in fact, it's getting worse all the time." [2]

Bernie sat quietly for a moment, smiling. He almost seemed to be laughing at us — though maybe I was just being paranoid. More than a few of those beliefs struck a chord with me. In fact, I agreed with most of them! No wonder we were near bankruptcy. No wonder I was deep in debt.

"Any of these beliefs sound familiar?"
That was a rhetorical question if I ever heard one.

"All right, you've taken the first step toward changing that belief, for once you've consciously identified a core belief, you can begin to consciously change it. *For limiting core beliefs aren't true in themselves, only our thinking makes them so.*

"Everyone who's not succeeding at something has a great many reasons to justify their lack of success — and their reasons are valid, because they're obviously true for them at present.

"Now, take a moment, and reflect on this: It doesn't matter what has happened to you in the past — what matters *now* are the particular dominant core beliefs you accept and carry around with you, because these beliefs completely influence your behavior and your life experience.

"Core beliefs are self-fulfilling prophesies."

He paused, giving those words even more emphasis.

"If you believe *it's so hard to succeed,* you'll certainly have a difficult time doing it. You might never even try. Even if you try something, you'll only work against yourself, in some ways, and ultimately fail. And this failure in turn becomes another reason to support your belief that *it's so hard to succeed.* Everyday we see the confirmation of our beliefs. The world and everyone in it seems to act in accordance with our beliefs. *Always.*

"It's all summed up in a saying on a magnet on my refrigerator:

> *"If you believe you can,*
> *or if you believe you can't,*

you're right.

"Henry Ford said that. He knew what he was talking about."

CHANGING YOUR CORE BELIEFS

"How can we change our limiting core beliefs? It's quite simple, surprisingly simple for those of us who think any process of change has to be difficult, or complex, or mysterious, or painful."

He said the next words with quiet passion.

"First, you have to accurately identify the core belief, in the simplest possible words. Then you gradually discard it by repeatedly affirming, with emotional conviction, a new belief that contradicts the old one and works better for you.

"That's the essence of the 'core belief process'. You'll probably need to repeat this process several times, dealing with the same issues and same beliefs, but eventually, your old limiting beliefs change for the better. You'll know the core beliefs have changed when your experiences change and you see definite improvements in your life.

"I heard a good example of this process the other day. A tennis coach was working with a professional player who was very good at the game — except when it reached match point, and then his game would fall apart.

"The coach said, 'I have an affirmation for you that'll really improve your game.' The player expected something profound or inspiring. The coach said, 'Repeat to yourself, at least twenty-five times a day, *I love match points.*'

"The player said, 'But I *hate* match points!'

"The coach insisted he try it, and he did, even though he felt the affirmation wasn't at all true. His game improved immediately — and eventually, he even found he *loved* match points."

THE CORE BELIEF PROCESS

"Now, I said the core belief process is simple — and the basic concept *is* simple: discover a core belief and find an affirmation to replace that old belief with a better one. It's a simple concept, but *doing it* can be difficult.

"Sometimes it's a challenge to discover those core beliefs — *and* put them in simple words that get to the heart of the problem we're creating for ourselves. Core beliefs can be elusive, especially for those of us who tend to intellectualize a great deal — the 'rampant rational mind' type — or for those who tend to get engulfed in overwhelming emotions — the 'rampant emotional' type. Now, there's certainly nothing wrong with either our rational minds or our emotions, but the two need to be balanced, in harmony. If one dominates the other, we lose touch with our natural, innate clarity, and create many more problems for ourselves than necessary.

"Whenever we're emotionally upset, it can be especially difficult to identify the core belief that's operating. Yet that's exactly when this process is most effective — when we're upset and agitated about something, or following a disturbing event that remains unresolved.

"You can do the process alone, or with a partner. If you do it with a partner, one of you should ask the questions while the other answers, taking just a few minutes for each question. If you do it alone, answer the questions silently or, even better, out loud to yourself, or you can write down your answers to each question, or record it and play it afterward.

"I wish more people knew about the core belief process. It's cheap therapy. It's the best kind of therapy, because you can do it yourself. And it has results: rapid growth, empowerment. *Conscious evolution.*

"Let's do it right now.

"Sit quietly for a moment. Take a deep breath, and relax as you exhale.

"Then think of a particular situation, problem, or area of your life you want to improve."

All four of us probably thought of the same problem: *potential bankruptcy.*

"*Describe the nature of the problem, situation, or area of your life you want to work on.* Take about three or four minutes to think about it or talk about it in general."

I'd been thinking about it all week, from early morning to late in the evening. We had a big mess on our hands, and could be in deep doo-doo, as a certain beloved U.S. president used to say.

"*What emotions are you feeling?* Name the specific emotion, such as fear, anger, frustration, guilt, sadness. Don't describe any particular thoughts you are having about it at this point."

Fear. Anger. Frustration. Guilt. Sadness, too. I was feeling them all.

"*What physical sensations are you feeling?*"

I had a gnawing discomfort in my stomach, when I thought about it. No surprise that it was in my power center. These were power issues. I had tension in my neck and back and shoulders as well — I was uptight!

"*What are you thinking about?* What conditioning or programming can you identify? What tapes are running in your head? What negative thoughts, fears, or worries are you having? Take a few minutes to describe your thoughts."

Bernie sat quietly. I was worried about losing my business, the source of my livelihood, as well as that of five other people who were all good friends. The bottom might drop out — that phrase had come to mind many times over the week. I could have gone on and on, but Bernie kept it fairly short.

"*What's the worst thing that could happen in this*

situation? What's your greatest fear? If that happened, then what would be the worst thing that could happen? What if that happened? What would be the *very* worst thing that could possibly happen? This question brings your deepest fears to light."

Bankruptcy. Then despair and destitution. Then death. A slow, painful death, with no friends, no one around me. What could be worse? Agony, panic. A living hell.

"*What's the best thing that could possibly happen?* What's the way you would ideally like it to be? What's your ideal scene in this area of your life?"

The best-case scenario was, for some reason, harder to picture than the worst-case scenario. It took me a while to imagine it: The business has explosive growth, and becomes solidly profitable. We all get rich, doing what we love to do. I become *a king in his generativity* — a phrase I'd heard somewhere recently that really surprised me when it sprang to mind.

"*What fear or negative belief is keeping you from creating what you want in this situation?* Once you've explored this, write your negative belief in one sentence, as simply and precisely as you can. If you have more than one, write them all down."

We scrambled for pens and paper. I wrote: *I'm afraid I'll*

fail. I'm afraid I don't have what it takes to succeed.

"Put it in the form of a belief — *I believe that I'm inadequate . . . I believe it's so hard to make money.*"

Those words certainly rang a bell. I wrote them down just as Bernie said them.

"*Now, create an affirmation to counteract and correct the negative belief.* It should be short and simple, and meaningful to you. *I am enough. I am worthy. I deserve to be successful!*

"It should be in the present tense, as if it's already happening. *I now have abundance in my life.* Or, *I am now creating abundance in every area of my life.*"

Bernie's words were again totally appropriate for me. I wrote down his suggestions.

"Your affirmation should be the *opposite* of your negative core belief. Turn the negative, limiting thought into a positive, expansive one. Some examples:

"Negative belief: *I don't have enough time to do the things I want to do.*

"Affirmation: *I have plenty of time to do the things I want to do.*

"Negative belief: *I have to struggle to survive.*

"Affirmation: *I am creating total success in an easy and relaxed manner, in a healthy and positive way.*

"Negative belief: *I'm under a lot of stress at work;*

it's unavoidable in my high-pressure job.

"Affirmation: *I now relax and enjoy myself at work, and accomplish everything easily.*

"Negative belief: *Money corrupts people.*

"Affirmation: *The more money that comes into my life, the more power I have to do good for myself, for others, and for the world.*

"Negative belief: *The world is a dangerous place.*

"Affirmation: *I now live in a safe, wonderful world.*

"Negative belief: *It's so hard to have a loving, on-going relationship.*

"Affirmation: *I now have a loving, on-going relationship, in an easy and relaxed manner, in a healthy and positive way.*

"You get the idea. Write down your affirmation."

I wrote: *I am now creating success in an easy and relaxed manner, in a healthy and positive way.* It was strangely frightening and wonderful at the same time to put those words on paper.

"*Say or write your affirmation repeatedly, over a period of several days.* Repeat your affirmation silently to yourself, while relaxing. Picture everything working out exactly as you want it to.

"Write your affirmation down and put it where you'll see it often.

"Write it ten or twenty times a day, if necessary, until you feel you've absorbed it as a positive core belief. Go ahead and write it a few times, now. If negative thoughts come up, write those thoughts on the back of the paper, then keep writing the affirmation on the front until it feels free of any emotional resistance.

"That's the entire core belief process."[3]

We wrote our affirmations. Plenty of negative thoughts came up — for all of us. We scribbled away while Bernie sat serenely. When he finally started speaking, he was back to that quiet, hypnotic voice, punctuated by silences.

"Feel free to play with this process and modify it to suit your own particular needs.... Change the words of your affirmation as often as you want. I've seen it have a profound and positive effect on a great many people, including myself....

"All you need is a willingness to be honest with yourself. Your spontaneous answers to the questions might surprise you. After going through this process, most people experience a wave of relief, as if we're feeling a lot *lighter*. It's as if we'd been carrying around an emotional weight on our shoulders, one we weren't even fully aware of, and we've suddenly let it go. The result can be exhilarating."

I didn't feel exhilarated, but I did experience a sense of relief as I wrote my affirmation. I felt hopeful, for the first time all week. I am creating success, in my own unique way. The road will undoubtedly have its ups and downs, its bumpy patches, but I am moving, day by day, toward my ideal scene.

This is what I affirm.

THE POWER OF AFFIRMATIONS
AND VISUALIZATION

"When you do the core belief process, you'll discover that the right affirmations can have a deep and positive effect on you ... they can change your life, in fact. *Affirmations are the single most powerful tool we have for creating what we want in life, for they can literally change our negative core beliefs into positive ones.*

"There's nothing difficult or esoteric about doing affirmations; it's a natural process we're doing all the time, sometimes consciously, more often unconsciously.

"The word *affirmation* comes from the Latin word *affirmare,* which means *to make firm.* Affirmations literally 'make firm' the reality we desire.... How can this be?"

He paused, for a long time, almost as if he expected one of us to answer his question. We just sat in silence, once again lulled into a sense of calm and quiet by the intense near whisper of his voice.

"We're naturally creative beings.... In the broadest, deepest sense, we have all created our present life situation. We create our own experience of reality, though most often we do it subconsciously. We create the life situations that we feel, in some way, we deserve. The core beliefs we accept about ourselves lead us subconsciously to create the life we're living....

"How *do* we create something? How do we write a book or knit a sweater? How do we repair a leaky sink or fill a living room with furniture? First, we develop an *intention* to do something, that is, we *affirm* to ourselves we're going to do it. 'I'm going to write a book.... I think I'll knit a sweater.... I've got to fix that leaky faucet.... We need some living room furniture....' All these are affirmations, words that *make firm* your intention to do something.

"Once the intention is firm, we summon the creative power of our mind and visualize the results. An affirmation always contains a visualization of some kind within it. We do this so often the process is usually automatic, subconscious.

"Both our conscious, linear, verbal mind and our sub-conscious, intuitive, spontaneous mind have the power to visualize results. When visualization is done repeatedly, and when it's supported by our mental and physical energy, we create exactly what we're affirming and visualizing....

"Now, *visualizing* doesn't necessarily mean literally see-ing the final results in actual form in our mind's eye, though this sometimes happens. Different people visualize in differ-ent ways. When you say, for example, 'I'm going to the store for some milk and cookies,' this simple statement involves both an affirmation and a visualization: You 'see' yourself going to the store, in some way — you imagine what's involved in going to the store — and you affirm that you'll do it by your statement, whether it's spoken out loud or just a thought in your mind. Your affirmation and visualization direct you to move in a certain direction, and you create your desired reality — in this case, milk and cookies.

"We're constantly visualizing and affirming, but too often we do it unconsciously in a way that creates negative results. Many of our words and thoughts reflect core beliefs we developed at an early age — *I can't do this; I'm incapable; this is too hard for me to handle; I don't know how; I'm not that talented; I'm unattractive;* and so on.

"Our core beliefs are also a result of the barrage of negativity from the media and from other people — *the world is a mess; it's so hard to succeed; it's so hard to find the right person; I need something else to make me happy;* and so on. Endlessly.

"It's unfortunate, but these ideas, whether they're spoken out loud or hardly noticed inner dialogue, are powerful affirmations — so powerful they create the reality we're affirming. . . .

"Fortunately, it's not that difficult to overcome even a lifetime of negative self-conditioning. All it takes is the desire to change, an understanding of the process, and perseverance. When you find yourself thinking negative thoughts, or saying negative things, replace those old limiting words with new, positive words. Start seeing yourself as strong and capable and creative, surrounded by opportunities — infinite possibilities! As you support positive core beliefs, they eventually replace the old, worn-out ones, and your life becomes much more enjoyable. . . .

"In *Illusions*, Richard Bach wrote, *Argue for your limitations and they are yours.* How true! Focus on your strengths instead, and they become yours. Focus on your innate talents and creativity — we all have unique talents and skills, when we think about it. *We're all creative geniuses,* in some absolutely original way. We all have some unique contribution we can make to the world. Focus on your dreams, and they become your reality. . . .

"I've said James Allen's words before, but they're worth repeating, again and again, because they're so powerful: *You will become as great as your dominant aspiration.... If you cherish a vision, a lofty ideal in your heart, you will realize it.*

"For years, I've had that quote on the wall in my office, in big, bold letters. It's a constant reminder, a powerful, self-fulfilling affirmation: *I cherish a vision, a lofty ideal in my heart, and I am now realizing it.*

"How much better to let words like these guide our lives, rather than words of limitation.... You can do whatever you want in life — all you need is the key to realizing your own 'vision and lofty ideals'. That key is your power to affirm and visualize, a power you've always had....

"You've been looking for something for years, and you find it's something you already had, all along...something you've been using, all along, though just not too effectively at times."

He smiled at that.

"There's a famous metaphorical story from Tibet: A woman dreams she's lost her head. The dream is so vivid that she gets up and rushes around frantically trying to find it. She searches everywhere, until she meets someone who simply holds up a mirror to her, and she sees that she had it all the time, and losing it was only a dream...."

We sat in silence for awhile.

WATCH WHAT YOU SAY!

"When you start to work consciously with affirmations, you naturally become much more aware of *every word you say* — and you eventually become aware of almost every negative thought that drifts through your mind.... So many of the habitual phrases we repeat to ourselves or others have the power to limit us and prevent us from creating what we want in life. As you do affirmations consciously, you become aware of all these phrases — and as you let them go, out of your speech and thought, your life improves *dramatically....*

"So many people constantly repeat negative, limiting thoughts and words, and then wonder why their lives are a mess: 'This job is killing me... that just makes me sick... oh, my aching back... that guy's a pain in the neck... I *hate* this' ... and so on. These words, like all words, send powerful messages to your subconscious mind. Watch what you say; words have a great deal of power, for good and for ill.

"As Margaret Atwood wrote, *A word after a word after a word is power.*"

OVERCOMING FEAR OF FAILURE

"If you're courageous enough to actually *do* the core belief process — and it takes courage — you'll probably find you have a *fear of failure.*

"Every successful person I've ever known or heard of, including myself, has experienced failure before they became successful. Failure serves an invaluable purpose: *it creates the foundation for success.* Failure is far more educational than success, because we learn more with every failure than we do with success. Every failure I've had has contributed to my success. My failures are the cost of my education — and education is essential and ongoing."

Bernie broke into a broad grin.

"I remember a profound bit of conversation I heard years ago on the old *Amos 'n' Andy* TV show. Amos — or Andy, I forget which — says to Kingfish,

"'Kingfish, where'd you get your good judgment?'

"And Kingfish says, 'From my experience.'

"'And where'd you get your experience?'

"And Kingfish says, 'From bad judgment.'

"Failure, and the bad judgment that precedes it, are necessary ingredients in creating success. *It's okay to fail.* Everyone who has ever tried something new has done it, repeatedly. Look at a child beginning to walk. Every one of us who learns to walk has had our share of falls and bumps and bruises.

"Someone once used this analogy: A pilot flying a plane is off course ninety-nine percent of the time. But the pilot just keeps correcting, and correcting, over and over. When we go off course, we sometimes fail — but our failures eventually teach us how to succeed. Success happens easily and effortlessly when you are physically, emotionally, mentally, and spiritually aligned. Every failure shows us that, in some way, we're out of alignment. So then we correct ourselves, and get back on course.

"George Bernard Shaw said it very well: *A life spent in making mistakes is not only more honorable but more useful than a life spent doing nothing....*"

We thought about that for a while.

"*The only real failure is in quitting.* As long as what you do is aligned with your mission or purpose in life, you don't need to fear failure, for you'll be shown step by step how to reach your goals. The experience you gain from your failures, miscalculations, and poor judgment will inevitably lead you to success, if you keep at it — with one exception, though, I should mention: If you waste your time and talent through addictive behavior, it's difficult, if not impossible, to truly succeed."

DEALING WITH ADDICTIONS

"Maybe I don't need to mention this to any of you. But maybe I do. If you need to hear it, you'll know it...."

He took a deep breath.

"I picked up a hitchhiker once who was pleasant, humorous, obviously intelligent. He said his car had recently been repossessed and, as we talked, he said he'd lost his job, his wife, his children, and his home because of his addiction to gambling at race tracks. He'd moved with his family from the East Coast to the West Coast in an attempt to quit gambling, but — surprise! — immediately found there was just as much opportunity to waste his money at racetracks in the west as in the east. He wasn't sure what he was going to do next; he had no idea how to get his life back together — and he was on his way to the race track, once again.

"All of us have seen how addictive behavior prevents people from getting what they want in life. Each one of us needs to honestly assess our lifestyle and habits, and see if any kind of addictive behavior is keeping us from achieving our goals and purpose in life. All the techniques for attaining success in the world will never work if we undermine ourselves through addictive or self-destructive behavior. Obviously.

One rule of thumb I discovered over the years: If you think you *might* have a problem with something, you probably *do* have a problem. If you don't have a problem, you never think about it, do you?

"Fortunately, there are plenty of choices we have to remedy the situation. The principles of Alcoholics Anonymous are brilliant; they're highly effective in resolving the problems created by addictive behavior.

"The twelve steps that are the basis of recovery in AA can be applied to any and all kinds of problems in our lives, whether the problem has anything to do with addiction or not.

"There are hundreds, thousands of other organizations and other philosophies, of course, that deal effectively with addictions and other mental and emotional problems. We all have access to them, and shouldn't hesitate to use their resources, if necessary. Some of the most brilliant and successful people in the world have had to wrestle with addictions. I have, too — so I know what I'm talking about."

He sat quietly after that little bombshell. When he spoke, he was even quieter than he had been. And somehow the way he talked — or perhaps the authority in his voice — forced us to concentrate on every word.

AN EXERCISE IN VISUALIZATION
AND AFFIRMATION

"Let's do a short exercise before we go. It's something I recommend doing often — four or five times a week. It takes only a few minutes each day, and can create positive results in your life in just a few weeks. I *promise* you this is true. . . .

"During these few minutes, *relax* . . . suspend all your critical, rational, or 'realistic' beliefs, and visualize your ideal scene, affirming that you already have it. This simple exercise can be used to create *anything* you desire: health, wealth, wisdom, happiness, serenity . . . a relationship, a peaceful environment . . . a new house, a new car, a good grade on a test, the solution to a problem, or whatever you want. . . ."

He closed his eyes, took a deep breath, and did the exercise with us as he talked us through it.

"Get comfortable, either sitting or lying down. Close your eyes. Take a few deep breaths, and relax thoroughly. . . .

"Take a deep breath, and as you exhale, *relax your body.* . . . Take another deep breath, and as you exhale, *relax your mind.* . . . Take another, and as you exhale, *let everything go* . . . all worry, all thought, all doubts....

"As you relax, enjoy the feeling of simply breathing, and simply relaxing...."

There was a long moment of silence. It felt good to relax....

"Now picture, as clearly and as detailed as you can, whatever you want to create. *Imagine your ideal scene as clearly as you can, as if you have already created it, and are enjoying it....* Picture as many details as possible....

"Spend a minute or two focusing on it, enjoying the imaginary scene you're creating."

Another moment of silence....

"Now, find an affirmation that nourishes and supports your visualization, and repeat it to yourself, over and over. An example might be, *Every day in every way, I am getting better and better...* or even, *I now have an income of x dollars per year.*

"A more expansive affirmation could be *I now have a beautiful home that I pay for easily and effortlessly, with lots of land, views of nature, and a large quiet studio where I create works of art that bring me over $250,000 a year in income, easily and effortlessly. So be it — so it is!*"

He sat in serene silence while we found our affirmations. I came up with one that felt good: *Our company is now growing and flourishing, easily and effortlessly. We are creating wonderful success.*

"Take a moment to enjoy and savor whatever 'fantasy', whatever *vision* you've created. Add a few more details, and play with your visualization, until it *feels* as if it already exists in the world.

"Finish by taking one more deep, relaxing breath and affirm to yourself, *This, or something better, is now manifesting for the highest good of all concerned. So be it — so it is!*"

We sat in silence for a long time. He had quietly induced a meditative state in all of us. I felt comfortable, soothingly relaxed. We would have sat in total silence for as long as Bernie did, without even thinking it was at all unusual.

"Open your eyes and come back to the present moment, feeling refreshed and relaxed, feeling the happiness and contentment that comes from achieving what your heart desires...

"Repeat this exercise, focusing on the same thing, at least four or five times a week, preferably every day. Soon — within two or three weeks — you'll have absorbed your visualization deeply into your subconscious, and you'll begin to see results in your life. Some exciting 'coincidences' will start to happen. Barriers will crumble. You'll meet someone or hear something that'll help you take a great leap forward. You'll find yourself moving *inexorably* toward the manifestation of your vision.

"In some cases, we're visualizing goals that'll probably take years to reach, yet we'll still see some concrete results quite quickly. The first small, achievable steps to take will become obvious: perhaps you'll start a new creative project, or have a brainstorm and realize how to make far more money. There are infinite possibilities! As you continue to visualize your ideal scene, you'll be led, step by step, to its fulfillment.

"If you don't see results in a reasonable amount of time, it means you're blocking yourself in some way. Go back to the core belief process and find out what beliefs are limiting you, preventing you from getting what you want, and *deserve*, in your life.

"This technique of conscious visualization and affirmation is very simple, it's true — it might even seem *too* simple to some people. But after using these tools awhile, you'll see how effective they are. And you'll become much more aware of what you're thinking and what you're picturing for yourself *every moment throughout the day* — even in your dreams.

"By imagining and affirming what you want in life, repeatedly, you open the gates to the *limitless* power of your creative imagination.

"I have found this to be true in my own experience, and I challenge you to try a similar experiment on yourself."

I went home a changed person. The problems at work, while still severe, were no longer overwhelming emotionally. I felt as if I had a powerful tool to deal with the problem: the tool of visualization and affirmations.

I hoped I could remember Bernie's words when Monday morning rolled around, with all its problems and challenges.

The rain had started to fall. Instead of being irritated by it, as I had been so often before, I saw it for what it was: a blessing for the earth, nurturing all of life with sacred water, helping everything grow. Even me.

KEY SEVEN

Practice the Fine Art of Communication

As a being of power, intelligence, and love, and the lord of your own thoughts, you hold the key to every situation, and contain within yourself that transforming and regenerative agency by which you may make yourself what you will.

— James Allen, *As You Think*

The situation at work didn't get worse during the next week, as I had feared, and it didn't get better, as I had hoped. Apparently my hopes and fears just about equally balanced each other, because we were in a holding pattern.

I kept affirming it would all work out for the highest good

of all concerned, in an easy and relaxed manner, in a healthy and positive way. But I also kept struggling, trying to survive, trying unsuccessfully to get our product out of the distributor's warehouse. I was frustrated and angry — and felt I was completely justified in feeling that way. I did the core belief process three times during the week, and could have done it every day. Each time was during a fairly intense emotional experience, and each time my feelings shifted afterward. The problems didn't go away, but my *reactions* to them changed, at least for a while. What will be will be, I thought. There's a reason for everything. If I'm a dismal failure, I'll learn a lot in the process. I'll learn what not to do next time.

It was true: It was all part of my education. It was good to be working with Bernie's words at the time. I loved going home at night and transcribing the tapes. They filled me with hope.

Bernie came back the next Friday to meet with us once more as a group. Again, four of us showed up and two didn't. I wished the other two would hear what Bernie had to say, but they weren't interested. It certainly didn't make a bit of difference to Bernie whether they showed up or not. So I just let it be. They'd learn and grow in their own way.

We gathered our chairs around again, and Bernie sat on his funky throne, serene as usual, amused by it all.

"You know, when five of us sit around like this, we form a pentagon, a five-pointed star, with each of us sitting at a point. It's a powerful symbol of creation, of manifestation, a symbol of the star we originated from.

"In every meeting you have, whether business or family, try to sit in a circle, and imagine you're forming a star, with as many points as the number of people in the group. Imagine you're each a part of the star, in your unique way. Together, we all become stars, and fulfill our dreams."

He was adamant, dynamic, completely different from the week before.

"So much of our fulfillment depends on our relationships with others. Our relationships can be either the most satisfying or the most frustrating things in our lives. And success is built on relationships. No one succeeds in a vacuum. Even artists or writers who work alone all day need agents, publishers, some kind of contact with the outside world to market their work. If your idea of success is living as a complete hermit, avoiding all contact with humanity, you might be an exception to the rule. But almost all of us need a network of relationships with others to reach our goals.

"Almost all of us want to have satisfying, healthy, honest relationships with those around us.

"Some people, it's true, have attained what appears to be success and yet have stressful, bitter relationships with the people they live and work with. But who really wants or needs that kind of stress? What good does it serve?

"It's sad but true that most of us have worked for people or have known people who have done well financially but have been miserable failures at having satisfying relationships with those around them. They just haven't been taught and don't understand something vitally important — the key to successful relationships: *effective communication.*"

The Seventh Key:
Practice the art of effective communication;
learn how to settle arguments.

"Communication is an art, and can be learned like any other art. This is a subject that should be taught in schools, but isn't — at least as far as I know — and most of us haven't been taught to communicate effectively, especially when we're angry, upset, or worried, or depressed.

"It's hard to express our feelings with others, especially when those feelings are negative. Most people don't even try to talk about their feelings — until their irritation grows into overwhelming anger that explodes and causes more anger, hurt, and guilt for everyone.

"This is sad, because there's another way to talk to each other, a way that minimizes alienation, and even brings us closer together, so we understand each other more deeply, and even discover a new kind of love and appreciation, rather than drift apart.

"Here's how it works."

He stopped and sipped his cappuccino. I'd never seen him so animated.

"In *any* kind of relationship — whether with families, friends, lovers, neighbors, employers, co-workers, professional associates, even international relations between countries — *everyone involved has the right, and must be given the opportunity, to speak their mind freely.* If the relationship is to work successfully, everyone has to have their say; otherwise, destructive feelings can develop, and fester and grow. Ultimately, hostile feelings and separation — even war! — results from this breakdown in communication.

"One of the most valuable things we can ever learn is how to communicate our feelings and offer our honest feedback without making people feel they've been attacked, or 'dumped on' — inundated with built-up resentment, anger, and criticism.

"There's a specific technique for this. It works best when you're in the middle of an argument, but you can use it in ordinary conversation, too, with great results."

THE ARGUMENT-SETTLING TECHNIQUE

"One of the best things about this technique is you can use it whether or not the other person is willing to go through it with you. To explain it clearly, though, I'll assume that both of you are aware of the technique and willing to use it. Once you understand how it works, you can modify it to use with an unwilling partner, or even intervene into someone else's argument and resolve it — something I've done many times. After all, everyone wins in the end, and that's the best part of successful communication.

"When you find yourself arguing with someone, or when you have something to say that's been bothering you, go through these six steps."

He counted the steps on his fingers, child-like, starting with his thumb.

"One: *Stop arguing.* Once you start arguing, you're getting nowhere. Nothing's ever been resolved in the heat of an argument.

"Have you ever heard anyone stop in the middle of an argument and say, 'You know, you're right about that. I'm changing my mind.' It never happens. Both of you are trying so hard to be heard that neither one is open to hearing what the other's trying to say. Everyone's shouting and no one's listening! Arguing compounds the problem. It doesn't solve it; it only makes things worse. So just make a decision to stop arguing and abide by the rules of the game.

"Remember, it takes two to tangle. If you refuse to argue, the argument won't continue for long.

"Two: *Let the other person completely express*

themselves, without interrupting them, and without denying what they're saying, defending yourself, or putting yourself or the other person down in any way.

"Just listen to what the other person is saying, and take it in, and accept it as being exactly what they need to say at that moment.

"This is the most challenging step, because it's so hard not to interrupt or react negatively. But it's also the most important step, because it lets the other person express their feelings without interruption. It also teaches you to hear criticism and hear someone's frustration and anger without immediately reacting — and this is an *extremely* valuable skill to gain.

"When you go through this process the first time, you'll probably find it difficult — almost *agonizing* — not to interrupt. But that's the key to the effectiveness of this technique: It's *essential* that you learn to listen without interrupting.

"If the other person is especially angry, if difficulties between you have built up for a long of time, they'll probably throw a lot of different feelings and issues at you that you, out of habit, want to respond to *immediately.*

"It's hard to even remember everything that's coming at you — when I first did this process, I had a notebook, and made quick notes of what was said, so I could remember to respond to every point. Later I realized it wasn't necessary at all to respond to everything. It's all right to take notes, as long as you keep listening and *don't interrupt* — and don't deny what they're saying, defend yourself, or put yourself or the other person down in any way, not even through unspoken body language. Just sit there and hear what they're saying, without responding. The other person will always finish what they have to say in a surprisingly short amount of time — a few minutes or so — though it might not *feel* like a short time to you.

"Three: *Now it's your turn to express your thoughts and feelings, as completely as possible, and the other person has to be quiet and listen, without interrupting you.* Encourage the other person to hear what you're saying without denial or defense, without putting you or anyone else down in any way.

"If the other person interrupts — and at first they probably will — remind them that you listened without interrupting, and you want them to do the same thing. They'll get another turn in just a minute.

"Take as much time as you need. Once you can speak without being interrupted, it takes just a few minutes for each person to 'blow off their steam' and say everything they have to say.

"After you've finished, the first person usually wants to respond, and at that point, the second and third steps may be repeated as many times as necessary — they speak, then you speak, *without being interrupted* — though it's very rarely necessary to repeat these steps more than two or three times.

"Before long, you find the air clearing between you — I've *never* known this to fail, if you've been able to listen and speak without interruption.

"You realize how the constant interruptions of your earlier arguments kept fueling those arguments. When you stop interrupting each other and listen instead, the heat of the argument vanishes — the anger disappears.

"Now you can move on to the next step:

"Four: *Ask the other person what they want from you, and give them the time and encouragement, without interrupting, to tell you exactly what they want and need.* Listen and remember. Every argument is based on the fact that the people involved aren't getting what they want. Then:

"Five: *Tell the other person exactly what you want from him or her.* Be as honest and direct as possible. Make it as clear as possible.

"Now you're ready for the final step:

"Six: *Negotiate with each other. Make clear agreements that work for both of you.* Compromise may be necessary for one or both of you, but keep negotiating, until you reach an agreement you're both satisfied with: a *win-win* agreement.

"You might have to do some creative brainstorming to come to an agreement, you might have to be flexible, you might have to give something up, but in almost every case you can find a creative solution that works for *both* of you.

"Simple enough?"
He broke into a broad smile, on the verge of a laugh, and said, "Simple to explain. Not easy to do. But it *works.*"

WHY THE ARGUMENT-SETTLING TECHNIQUE WORKS

"Why does it work so effectively? I can think of several reasons, some I mentioned, some I haven't:

"When arguments start, we stop listening. The frustration builds, for everyone involved, and we say things that only make matters worse, things we usually regret later. As the argument builds, our anger builds. Covert, cutting remarks become overt, negative criticism or just downright stupid, thoughtless, angry things you don't even really mean. No one likes anger or criticism directed at them. It's natural to respond with self-defense and anger. By using this technique, you get the satisfaction of expressing your feelings in a way that they're *heard* — and anger and frustration dissolve.

"When you use this technique, you can't get away with the all-too-common reactions of denial, defense, or putting yourself or someone else down. You're forced to listen to what the other person is saying. You're forced into a more mature and intelligent response — a *wiser* response, one that comes from a higher level of consciousness, if you will, one that teaches you to be more open to other people's opinions and feelings, and helps you grow as an individual.

"You don't have to agree with what they're saying. You're completely free to disagree if you feel, for any reason, that what they're saying isn't appropriate for you. But you have to at least be willing to hear it, and take a moment to consider it without immediately reacting, and realize they have a right to their feelings and opinions, just as you have a right to yours. This takes the steam out of an argument, in a surprisingly short time."

He was adamant as he spoke.

"When you learn to listen to others, without interrupting or defending yourself, another great thing happens: You start to *empathize* with other people, to see why they feel what they feel, and to understand them better and even sympathize with them. You gain insight into the tremendous diversity of human beings, with all our human feelings, with all the fascinating complexity of human relations. You come to understand that we all see things very differently. You find yourself broadening, gaining much more experience — the experience of another person's perspective. You gain a great deal of knowledge and, eventually, wisdom.

"And you discover, through experience, that *almost any problem can be solved in a way that allows everyone involved to win.* It's the partnership model. It may take quite a bit of negotiation, creative thinking, maybe even compromise. It may involve breaking what seem like major problems down into smaller, more specific problems. You may have to agree to forgive and forget the past and go on from there and make clear agreements for the future. You may have to let go of something. But there is almost always a solution to be found that works for everyone involved.

"Once you understand it and work with it, this little technique is a powerful tool for communication, and for your own evolution. Because that's what happens when we learn how to listen, and how to stop fighting and resolve arguments: we grow, we *evolve.* We come to see things more clearly. We become more skillful, more effective. Wiser, more powerful. Life becomes more enjoyable — it's far more fun to be a lover than a fighter. It's healthier, and you live a lot longer."

He paused and smiled again. He seemed to be enjoying himself.

"Once you do this technique, you see how to use it with people who don't even know you're using it. If you get into an argument, you simply stop and say, 'Look, this argument is getting us nowhere. Arguing will not solve the problem. I'm going to sit here and listen to everything you have to say — *without interrupting you* — and then I'm going to ask you to listen to what I have to say, without interrupting me — okay?' They'll almost always agree, because all they really want is *to be heard.*

"Then let them have their say; let them release their pent-up frustration, without denying it or being defensive in any way. Again, it's absolutely essential you *don't interrupt* — the power of this technique is completely dependent on learning to listen without interrupting. Wait until they're finished.

"Then say, 'All right, I listened to you. Now I'm asking you to listen to me, and not interrupt until I'm finished. Then I'll listen to you again, *without interrupting*. Okay?'

"In this way, you can go through every step with them, even if they never agreed to go through it in the first place."

He sat quietly for a moment, grinning.

FEEDBACK AND PERSONAL POWER

"When you use this technique, you learn something else that's extraordinarily valuable: the importance of the feedback you receive from others. You'll probably find when you go through it that your natural impulse when you hear something you don't like is to deny it, defend yourself, or put yourself or others down in some way. To simply allow yourself to hear what others are saying, and to consider it without reacting to it, is difficult at first, unless you're very close to enlightenment.

"If we can change our attitudes about the feedback we receive from others, this *open listening* can become easy, even enjoyable. A more intelligent attitude is this: *Almost everything anyone says to us is useful in some way.* We might not like it, we might not agree with it, we might not accept it as being true, but there's some useful information in almost everything that's said to us.

"Once you do your affirmations and develop the core belief that you're a talented and worthwhile person, someone who has something to contribute to the world — which is certainly true — you find you naturally feel confident and clear when relating to friends, relatives, co-workers, everyone. You find you can listen to everything they have to say, accept the fact that they're speaking what they believe to be true, and usually discover something worthwhile in what they're saying. You may not agree with them, but you can definitely be open to hearing what they have to say.

"*This is the attitude of a powerful person,* a person who isn't threatened by others and doesn't have to deny, defend, or apologize."

AGREEMENTS, COMMITMENTS, AND NEGOTIATION

"One reason this technique works is that it ends with negotiation that results in clear agreements and commitments. You ask what they want from you, and you tell them what you want from them. These negotiations, in the long run, serve everyone. Agreements and commitments are essential in life, yet so many people are afraid of making them. So many people are afraid of the negotiation process in general!

"Yet, there's nothing to fear in negotiation, or in agreements and commitments, as long as the goal is to create a win-win situation for everyone involved.

"I used to feel completely uncomfortable negotiating almost anything — whether personal needs or business activities, *especially* involving money. I came to realize somewhere along the way that this fear of negotiation — like all fear — reflected some limiting core beliefs: I felt I wasn't good enough, in some way, or I didn't deserve to get what I wanted, for some reason. After working with the core belief process and the argument-settling technique, all that changed. Negotiation became *enjoyable*. Negotiation presents us with the challenge to creatively find ways for everyone to win.

"If you have difficulties negotiating — or making clear agreements or commitments — take a good look at your beliefs about yourself and your world. Work with the core belief process, until you're skillful and creative in your negotiations. You'll become far more effective, far more powerful, able to get what you want, and contribute far more to others and to the world."

He sat in silence for quite a while. He looked down at the floor, either thinking or meditating. Nobody moved. Then he asked, "Any questions?" There were none.

"Good. I'm gonna go home and sit in the hot tub."

KEY EIGHT

Listen to the Voice
of Your Intuition

Every night and every morn
  Some to misery are born
Every morn and every night
  Some are born to sweet delight...
We are led to believe a lie
  When we see not through the eye

— T.S. Eliot

Over two weeks passed, with no word from Bernie. We did the argument-settling exercise a few times, and Bernie was right: it worked wonders. We became a more united team. It was obvious we all had the same goal: a successful business that supported everyone.

Why had we allowed so many conflicts to fester, why were we working against each other? It had been such a waste of time and energy.

Another fascinating thing happened after I did the exercise a few times, one I'm somewhat embarrassed to mention for some reason: I began to fantasize having an intimate relationship with someone, in a way that could work for both of us. I knew I needed to do more inner work first. But I felt, with the argument-settling technique and the core belief process, I had two great tools for building a relationship. When I was ready, the right person would appear. And all would unfold easily and effortlessly. At least that became a fantasy, and it kept recurring.

The problems at work were still in a holding pattern. We kept surviving, but barely, as we tried to work out the basic conflict, and get our inventory out of the warehouse. There was no resolution in sight.

Bernie finally called and invited me to come out to his house. He said to come fairly late, after sunset; I drove over the next night.

We sat outside, in his favorite spot behind the house, and sipped a blend of fruit juice. "It's Kern's Guava and Koala Kiwi-Lime-Grapefruit," Bernie explained. It was carbonated, and tasty.

"It's the secret of my good health — fruit juice. I eat everything — I'm an omnivore. But I eat in moderation. I only eat when I'm hungry. And I start the day with fruit juice. It cleanses the system. I don't have any other breakfast, and I wait to eat lunch until I'm good and hungry. And if I have a heavy lunch, I only eat something light for dinner, like more fruit juice. Or a piece of pie, or some ice cream. Or jalapeno olives — I love olives stuffed with jalapenos! It cures what ails ya. Or nuts and raisins. Half my diet is probably cashews, raisins, and jalapeno olives. Health food.

"And I do a bit of yoga each day — at least a few *salutes to the sun.* And I meditate, nearly every day. And I sit in the hot tub almost every night. That's it — that's my health system.

"Maybe we should write a book about it: *The Elixir of the Gods Health System.* It's all based on fruit juice — the true elixir of the gods! You don't need to drink alcohol in the evening to relax — just have a blend of fruit juice, and sit in a hot tub and do a bit of meditation. Have some calming herbal tea if you want. You'll be wonderfully relaxed — and healthy." He toasted me with his glass of elixir.

Crickets were loudly playing their music, pulsing, almost electronic. The new moon had set right after the sun, and the night was pitch black, except for a canopy of shimmering stars.

"It's good to sit under the stars, every once in awhile, and just gawk at the universe," Bernie said. "And all we see is just one galaxy, average-sized, with about *two hundred billion* stars ... and there are at least *a hundred billion* other galaxies, in the known universe. ... "

We sat and gawked at the lustrous stars. Then Bernie motioned to me to turn my tape recorder on.

He began by quoting a poem:

"Every night and every morn
   Some to misery are born
Every morn and every night
   Some are born to sweet delight...
We are led to believe a lie
   When we see not through the eye

"Those words from T.S. Eliot are full of insight: 'We are led to believe a lie when we see not through the eye.'

"The eye is the eye of our innate intelligence, our understanding, knowledge, and wisdom; it's the inner eye of our vision, directly connected to our intuition.

"The lie we're led to believe is the lie of our negative, limiting core beliefs: the lie of our doubts and fears, the lie of hopelessness, the lie of failure. The lie that our lives leave so much to be desired; the lie that we aren't capable of being successful, fulfilled, happy...."

He spoke quietly over the crickets' song.

"The truth is *all* our fears are unfounded, ultimately, and our negative, limiting core beliefs are lies and distortions. The truth is we're intuitive, evolving people with hearts and minds capable of creating what we want in our lives...we're visionaries with magical powers, able to lead happy and fulfilled lives.

"This is true for others, and it's certainly true for you and me as well. We have all the tools we need to do it, to be it, and to have it. The source of our toolbox, our magical power, is within us, within our creative mind, within our intuition. It's a power we've always had — yet most of us have to search for it.

"In the core belief process, we focused on our emotions. What we were feeling, and what was that feeling telling us? Now we focus on our emotions again, but shift that focus in a different direction: Now we'll look at our emotions as *the gateway to our intuitive guidance.*

"The core belief process gives us a key to deal with our limiting beliefs and feelings. Now we'll look at a key that takes us beyond all limitations: *our intuition,* the calm, clear voice we all have within us that gives us access to limitless knowledge, wisdom, and power."

The Eighth Key:
Listen to the voice of your intuition,
and be aware of the ever-changing range
of your visionary emotions.

"Every emotion we feel — whether 'good' or 'bad' — joy, anger, contentment, depression, enthusiasm, fear, ecstasy, boredom, serenity, agitation, love, hate — *every* emotion has an important reason for being. Every emotion opens us up to our vast intuitive resources, and offers us the guidance we need in every moment. The more we're aware of our ever-changing range of emotions, the more intuitive information we receive.

"We all have 'gut feelings', intuitive hunches. To some degree, we're all psychic, able to tune into a vast amount of intuitive information about ourselves, about others, and our world. Information, knowledge, and wisdom come to us instantly, and we know the best thing to do in the moment."

He sat silently, for a long beat.

"Watch a child, an infant — watch the way emotions dance across a baby's face. They go from curiosity to radiant love, to fear, to frustration, to quiet gazing, to bliss — all in a few seconds. We still have that emotional child within us, a vitally important part of our multifaceted personality.

"How are you feeling right now? Take a moment, and answer."

It took me a moment to discover what I was feeling. I was content, yet restless in some way. I searched for the source of the restlessness, and some strange words popped into my mind: *I feel unborn, like a silent new moon.* I felt as if I had something to do, and I wasn't doing it. Something to be and I wasn't being it.

"Become more aware of your ever-changing range of emotions. And then try to act more consistently in a way that supports you emotionally. So many of us do things we don't like to do, or things that even violate us emotionally in some way. We work in a stressful job we don't like, or we spend our time with friends or relatives who are unsupportive, and undermine our confidence and dreams in some way....

"We need to support ourselves, and others, as much as we

possibly can, to do what's in harmony with our emotions. It isn't easy, but it's so rewarding when we do it. If we can be totally honest with ourselves, and willing to act on our feelings, we're guided, moment by moment, to create *the perfect life* for ourselves. To be all that we can be.

"Ultimately, just by doing what feels good, what feels right, in every moment, we're led step by step to the greatest success we can imagine. I almost always know, instantaneously, what choices to make, which projects to pursue, which ones to drop, what to do in every moment: If it feels exciting, if it feels good, I do it. If it doesn't, I don't. My feelings are my guide — and they're much more reliable than my rational, logical thinking processes, which are excellent tools, but can get me into trouble if they take me too far from my intuition."

He was silent for a moment.

"How do we connect with our intuition?

"Intuitively you know the answer to that question. I'm not being flippant, it's the truth. We all, in some way, already connect with our intuition. We can do it more often, if we make it a priority. Maybe we'll have to reflect on it awhile to hear it more clearly. But we all have an intuitive voice within us — usually we were much more conscious of it in our childhood. Do you remember?"

Yes, when I thought about it, I remembered a magical kind of awareness as a child. I remembered that I knew what I wanted to be when I grew up, and that it was an expansive dream, one I had long forgotten.

"Some people never lose touch with their intuition as they grow up. But most of us do, at least for a while, and have to rediscover it. There are many ways to do this. I can show you two: One is through simply understanding intuition, and the other is through meditation."

UNDERSTANDING INTUITION

"Where does a composer's music come from? Where does a great writer's novel come from? Where do the great scientific theories come from?

"Where do our 'first impressions' of people come from? Where do our 'gut feelings' and 'hunches' come from? Where does the feeling of comfort, or discomfort, come from the moment we're in a certain person's presence?

"From our intuition.

"We're all intuitive, and our intuition is active all the time. It's simply a matter of noticing it more clearly. It's one of our most important inner voices, but it's a calm, clear voice — even, in many people, a 'still, small voice within' — and it takes a quiet moment of attention to hear it.

"Our intuition is speaking all the time, but other, louder voices of fear and worry and rational thinking overwhelm it. Drinking too much alcohol or watching too much TV or listening to the radio or arguing with someone overwhelms the calm, clear voice of our intuition.

"It takes a moment of stillness to catch it. Some people naturally understand this, and do it easily, effortlessly. Others have to learn it. The voice of your intuition is directly connected with your feelings. Simply tuning in to your feelings tunes you in to the voice of your intuition — it's within all those feelings, somewhere."

He smiled; he was much calmer and quieter than he had been the last time. The next part was nearly a whisper.

"Our intuitive voice is always calm and clear. It's always supportive; it's always positive; it always *feels right*. It's a voice for our highest good, for the highest good of all concerned.

"Listen, and you will hear. It's always been there, and you've always known it. Connecting with our intuition is really a simple, natural process we've been doing all our lives. We just need to take a quiet moment to become aware of it."

We sat for a quiet moment.

MEDITATION

"Through meditation, you naturally become aware of the voice of your intuition — it's just one of the many good effects of meditation. There are many different forms of meditation, active and passive. Taking a walk alone can be a wonderful meditation. So can gardening, knitting, making things — anything where you're alone with your thoughts.

"One way to meditate is to sit in silence and just observe your thoughts — no more. When a thought arises, notice it, and then let it go. Sit and become aware of your thoughts."

We sat for a while in silence. It seemed like there was some crazed radio DJ in my head keeping up a constant patter of words. I even heard an obnoxious commercial! Bernie mercifully kept the silence short.

"Eventually, you'll become aware of the spaces between your thoughts. And you'll be able to sit in silence. But first, you have to still your mind...."

We sat some more. My mind was far from still. Some inner child sang an old nursery rhyme. Some critical parent told it to shut up.

"In silence, you become aware of the vast number of your thoughts — your mind churning out words.

"Just observe all your thoughts; don't judge them. You'll have all kinds of different internal voices, and you'll learn to identify them. You'll hear the agitated voice of fear. You'll hear skeptical voices, critical voices, probably asking, *Why am I sitting here? What am I doing? This is ridiculous. Nothing's happening. I'm wasting my time.*

"You'll hear efficient, rational voices, figuring out how to organize the rest of your day, or the next day, telling you you've forgotten something, or reminding you of things you need to do.

"Somewhere in there is a calm, clear voice: your intuition. Your intuition knows exactly why you're sitting there, and is infinitely happy you're doing it. Your intuition is supremely supportive of what you're doing. Your intuition knows who you are, underneath it all: a powerful, creative person with an important mission in life. Your intuition is there to help you fulfill your greatest dreams.

"You don't need to formally meditate — though it's certainly a good thing to do, for a great many reasons. All you need to do is sit quietly, for a brief period of time. Then do it again, and again.

"If you don't know what to do in a certain situation, just sit quietly for a moment, and then ask yourself what to do. Listen carefully to the answers that go through your mind. See how each one feels. Try it on for size.

"Notice the *emotion* behind those inner voices. Does that answer have an edge of fear? Or anger? If so, it's not your intuition. Does it feel calm and clear? Is it totally supportive of your highest good? If so, it's your intuition, guiding you as always with clarity and light."

We sat in silence again, for a long time. Maybe close to an hour, I had no idea. At some point the tape ran out. The sound of the crickets came and went, and when they quit zinging their tunes it was absolutely silent, except for the words in my mind.

Bernie sat with his eyes closed, looking supremely comfortable. He didn't move a muscle. I was able to relax at first, but had more and more discomfort as the hour rolled on, and had to wiggle my body and kick my legs. Time dragged on. I heard a great many inner voices, an endless litany of words, words, words. One voice said, *Is this all there is? Listening to my endless thoughts?* I felt I wasn't doing it right.

Finally, Bernie stretched, and seemed to have read my thoughts, for he said, "That's it. You did it. There's no right or wrong way to meditate. Just sit there and watch what happens." He stood up and gazed at the night sky.

"I wrote a poem once about intuition," he said. And he quoted from memory, quietly.[4]

> "*She's just a little girl, or a whispering old woman,*
>   *so shy in crowds or with loud talkers.*
> *She has a quiet little voice, delicate as a spider's web,*
>   *weaving her stories with an accent of stillness.*
> *Wait quietly for her, or she is gone.*

> "*Her songs are sung through luminous starlight,*
>   *her poems sparkle with the bright blood of life.*
> *Her words are yours, yours for the taking,*
>   *from her heart they have sprung,*
>   *to your heart they fly.*
> *Wait quietly for her, or she is gone.*

> "*A moment of her performance has changed many lives,*
>   *a minute of her presence makes life worthwhile.*
> *She has the power to guide us anywhere,*
>   *all doors are magically open to her.*
> *Wait quietly for her, or she is gone.*"

We waited quietly for a moment. An owl hooted once, twice, three times in the silence of the night, and then was gone.

KEY NINE

The Fine Art of Detachment

Make no appointments, and you'll have no dis-appointments.

— Swami Satchidananda

Two weeks passed, very quickly, before I heard from Bernie again. I transcribed his words on intuition, and hoped I was intuitively absorbing something as I did it.

I came home exhausted one night after an intense, stressful day, and felt I needed to do something different from my usual routine, though I didn't know what. I took a long, hot bath, then laid on my bed and relaxed. I was drifting close to sleep, but I asked this question to myself, to the universe: *How can I deal with these problems at work? What should I do?*

There was no answer. I relaxed more deeply, and asked again. This time an answer came, almost immediately: *You can't depend on what you can't control. Do what you can.*

And, in an almost visual way, I saw we'd been trying to change something that was completely beyond us to change. We couldn't rescue our distributor's company; they would have to resolve their own problems.

Instead, we should do what we could: focus on the things that had nothing to do with them. It should have been obvious to me much earlier, when I thought about it. We still had our direct mail, even though it was minimal; we still had other places where we sold our things that didn't involve that distributor. We needed to focus on what was already working, and develop it further.

These words came to mind: *God grant me the serenity to accept the things I cannot change, the courage to change the things I can, and the wisdom to know the difference.*

Where did that come from?

In spite of my intuitive insight, or whatever it was, things were still stressful at work. I finally decided to call Bernie; I was just reaching for the phone when it rang. "How about if we meet in my office next week?" he said. "I'll buy you lunch."

I was hoping we could meet sooner than next week, but Bernie, as usual, was in no hurry.

We sat again on the balcony overlooking the lobby — it was certainly the most unusual office I had ever seen, when I thought about it — and Bernie had his ham sandwich. We talked about all kinds of things, the weather, Bernie's last trip to Mexico. I mentioned the summer seemed to be flying by.

"I have a theory about that," said Bernie. "Remember how long summers were when you were in grade school?" I certainly did. "When you're two years old, a year is fifty percent of your life experience. When you're ten years old, it's ten percent of your life experience. When you're fifty, it's only two percent. So it's all relative. A summer for a kid really is much longer than it is for an adult. Time accelerates as you grow older. I'm eighty-three, so . . ."

"You're *eighty-three?*" I burst out. Bernie just laughed. "I don't believe it."

"I'll be eighty-four before long."

"You seem so . . . *young,*" I said — I couldn't find a better word.

"I *am* young," he said. "Age is a matter of mind — just like everything else. A matter of our beliefs. If you believe you'll age and fall apart at a certain time, you do. If you believe you can be young and strong at a hundred, you will be. The power of our beliefs is limitless."

The moment Bernie told me how old he was, my beliefs about the aging process completely changed. I used to think seventy was old. Now here was a healthy, supple, vital man in his mid-eighties. It blew my mind. All I could do was shake my head.

"You've got to keep moving, too. I do my yoga. And I dance, when I'm inspired."

And he got out of his chair and did a soft-shoe dance,

singing "Tea for Two," using "Do-do-do..." for all the words. He danced very well; he could have been on a vaudeville stage with that act. I don't know why I was surprised. He ended with a sweeping bow, and I applauded another side of a remarkable man.

Then he sat down and sipped his coffee and motioned to start the tape recorder, smiling so broadly it was difficult at first to talk.

"Okay. We've reached the ninth key..."

The Ninth Key:
Practice the fine art of detachment.

"I saw Swami Satchidananda speak once in San Francisco. What a handsome man! He's the Charlton Heston of gurus, you know. I just remember one thing he said — but it's been invaluable, over the years. He sat there in a lotus position, smiling, and he said, *Don't make any appointments, and you won't have any disappointments.*"

Bernie sounded and somehow looked like an Indian guru as he said it.

"For years after, whenever I felt disappointed about something I'd ask, *What appointments have I made here? What expectations do I have?*

"That simple phrase sums up a great truth that Buddha taught. I wish his teachings were better known in the West. Buddha is a very important figure in human evolution. He didn't teach a religion — he never said you had to *believe* anything he said — he taught psychology, a highly effective form of therapy. He taught that there were some simple yet *great* truths. One is that, yes, *life is suffering.* We can't deny it. Life is unfair. There's old age, sickness, and death. The existentialists are right; life is absurd. I saw a guy once with a T-shirt that said, LIFE IS A BITCH, AND THEN YOU DIE. That sums up Buddha's first great truth.

"But the existentialists — and most of the other Western philosophers and psychologists — never discovered Buddha's second great truth: *There's an end to suffering.* There's a state of being that's completely beyond suffering. A state of serenity and peace. A state of enlightenment.

"The third great truth is that *our suffering is caused by our expectations — our appointments.* It's been translated so many different ways. The important thing to understand is *the cause of our suffering is within us.* The world out there isn't doing it to us. We're doing it to ourselves, because of our expectations, our desire that the world be better in some ways, our emotion-backed demands that things be different from the way they are.

"It's been mistranslated and misunderstood by some people as *desire itself* — but our desire is not the problem.

Desires are natural, desires are *wonderful.* Desires are the driving force in our endless evolution. It's our *attachment* to those desires that causes the problem. It's when we can't accept things the way they are.

"I read a book published in India that put it this way: The cause of our suffering is *our thirst for permanence, our thirst for existence.* Now, of course, it's natural to thirst for existence: Every cell in our bodies literally thirsts for life! It's built into our genetic coding! We're like every other plant and animal on earth — we have a powerful life force within us that will fight to the last to survive. We're survivors! We're powerfully attached to life.

"And yet, we're all going to die — every plant and animal, at some time, makes that transition we call death. It's inevitable. At some point, we're forced to become detached from this life as we know it. At that point, all our other attachments to people, money, success, accomplishment, become irrelevant, and we learn what's truly important in life: how well we've *loved.* All else dissolves in an instant, the moment we make that transition we call death — it's really a *transformation* into a new form of life.

"It's good to reflect on these things, occasionally. It's good to face the undeniable fact of our mortality — at least the mortality of these physical bodies we love so much. It puts our lives into perspective. It can teach us the value of detachment. We're going to have to learn it sooner or later anyway....

"I'm always preaching the value of creating your ideal scene, making clear goals, and visualizing success. *The key to lasting happiness and fulfillment is to do these things — with passion — and yet be unattached to the results.* What will be will be.

"Learning detachment makes your life a lot easier. Relationships are smoother, because you're not insisting that other people have to change for you to be happy. Things are less frustrating in your work, and in your relationship with money, once you learn detachment.

"Look at money: There's a great book, *Letters to My Son*, by Kent Nerburn, that says something like this: 'Money rules our lives. You can't say it doesn't.... Yet it has nothing to do at all with what's important in life.'

"Here..." Bernie got up from his chair in a fluid motion. "That's too rough. I'll read it to you." He disappeared into his hotel room, and came out with a well-worn book.[5]

> *"Money rules our lives. You can say it doesn't. You can rail against it. You can claim to be above it or indifferent to it. You can do all the moral and intellectual gymnastics that you will. But when all is said and done, money is at the center of our very claim to existence.*
>
> *"Yet money is not of central importance. It has nothing whatsoever to do with the lasting values that make life worth living.*
>
> *"There, in a nutshell, is the dilemma. How do you reconcile yourself to something that is not important but is at the very center of your life?*

"Once you can understand that contradiction, you can see money for what it is, and learn to use it, and master it, without becoming a slave to it. You can set goals of exactly how much money you want to make, yet you can be detached too, because you know it's not really essential to your happiness and fulfillment.

"Money is essential to function in the world, for most people, yet it has nothing to do with what's really important in life.

"In your life, and in your business, it's important to make clear annual goals — and yet be detached from them as well.

"How do we do this? By *letting go emotionally* — accepting what's happening. And then wonderful things happen. The biggest problems dissolve. You have clear dreams of where you want to go, dreams you imagine over and over, and yet you enjoy every moment, here and now. You enjoy the journey as much as the destination. Each has its own absolute perfection.

"Keep visualizing, keep affirming that your goal is being created in an easy and relaxed manner, in a healthy and positive way, *in its own perfect time.* And be detached to the results. Enjoy yourself in the present moment, enjoy who you are, and what you have, enjoy the others around you.

"It's a matter of balance, as always, *the middle way,* as Buddha put it: You need to be passionate about your dreams, to desire your goals, but you also need to be detached to the results, to whatever unfolds day by day.

"If you get too passionate and desirous, you can get too attached to wanting certain results — and happiness will slip by you. You forget to enjoy the journey because you're always wanting to be at the destination.

"If you get too detached, you won't even bother to dream or make any plans, and you'll go nowhere. That's all right, of course, because you'll have discovered the key to happiness, and there's nothing else you need to do."

Bernie chuckled at that.

"One good way to learn detachment is to always affirm or pray to do God's will — whatever God means for you. At the top of your list of goals, put in big letters:

GOD'S WILL

"Whatever happens is God's will.

"There's a famous community in Scotland named Findhorn, where they did a great experiment: They planted two gardens. As they worked in the first one, they kept praying for big, beautiful vegetables, visualizing the finest plants they could imagine.

"In the second garden, they prayed only for God's will, and let it go at that.

"The first garden had magnificent fruits and vegetables — but the second garden had even greater ones, far bigger than people thought was possible to grow in that soil, so magnificent that Findhorn became famous for them.

"Keep praying to do God's will, and you'll probably be led far beyond your greatest dreams."

We sat in silence. The sounds of walking and the quiet hum of voices below turned into a piece of new music.

KEY TEN

Give Abundantly and Reap the Rewards — The Ten Percent Solution to Personal and Global Financial Problems

If universal charity prevailed,
earth would be a heaven
and hell a fable.

— Charles Colton

It was late in the fall. The pyracantha bush that had over-grown everything outside my window had exploded into bright red berries, and a mad flock of birds were attacking it wildly, getting drunk on fermented berry wine. The sun was bright and warm; it felt wonderful on my face. But I didn't have much time to enjoy the pleasures of a sunny day — I had to get to the office and take care of business.

Bernie called around noon, and quickly talked me into taking a walk with him behind his home. The work could wait.

The drive out into the country was beautiful. It had rained hard the night before; now leaves dazzled in the sun.

Bernie met me as I drove up. We both had a glass of water, then went out his back door, across the yard and onto a trail that wound for miles through the hills.

"We should get out and walk more," Bernie said. "Be more like Carl Sandburg. He said he needed to take long walks, so he could stop and sit on a rock and ask himself, *Who are you, Sandburg? Where are you going?*"

We walked on, over dry, golden grassy meadows that dipped down into cool areas shaded with oak and madrone and bay trees. We didn't talk for a long time. It was almost hot in the sun, that last autumn warmth you savor so much. It was cool in the shade, and I could feel winter coming on.

My thoughts wandered over many things. I thought of our meetings, over the spring and summer, and the book we were developing. And then I thought of a meeting we'd had a year or so ago, when he had told me about a Utopian novel he was writing, or at least thinking about writing.

I often thought about what he said that day. He envisioned a hugely successful nonprofit corporation whose mission was to get ten percent of the people and corporations in the world to donate at least five to ten percent of their income to help everyone, on every level of society — anyone who needs assistance in fulfilling their dreams.

It was a great, glorious vision of a world with a steadily increasing standard of living for everyone, propelled forward not by governments — though they were certainly part of the solution — but by the magical principle of *tithing.*

One person's vision could show us that it was possible to improve the world, even transform the world, and the key to it all was simply getting ten percent of the people and corporations to give away a small portion of their income. It was a remarkable vision, definitely worth pursuing.

When Bernie finally spoke, his words coincided with my thoughts.

"Remember that Utopian novel I was thinking of writing?"

"Sure."

"Well, I've changed my mind about it. I've found a much easier, simpler way. I don't have to write a novel. Utopian novels tend to be boring anyway. I just have to get *you* to put this in the last chapter of our book. And we probably don't need to start another nonprofit corporation — *the infrastructure is already in place.* There are thousands and thousands of nonprofits out there, and government agencies, and corporations, and churches, and schools, and individuals on their own that are already doing the work. All they need is more support.

"There are already thousands of kitchens feeding millions of people, and thousands of housing programs for the homeless. They just need far more support — volunteers as well as money — and there need to be more of them set up. There are millions of therapists and recovery centers out there; they just need more support, so everyone who needs them has access to them.

"There are already a vast number of schools at every educational level, they just need more money — *lots* of money

— so there is free public education again, from pre-school to grad school.

"There are already all kinds of organizations that support artists and entrepreneurial ideas, they just need more funding, more support — with time and energy and money.

"There are already all kinds of organizations protecting children and animals and the environment and indigenous peoples. They just need more support. The infrastructure is already in place. All we need to do is encourage more people to support it. All *we* need to do is make the concept clear to the world. Publish a book about it and get it noticed, get it read.

"Get corporations involved. Get schools involved. Get children saving and tithing, in schools around the world. Get at least ten percent of the world's population involved. That's the goal."

Bernie was speaking and walking quickly, even when our path wound sharply uphill. I was breathing heavily, my shirt damp with sweat.

The Tenth Key:
Give abundantly
and reap the rewards.
By doing so, we can transform
the world.

"The tenth and final key to creating the life you want is to give abundantly and reap the rewards. By giving, we can consciously help the world evolve into a sustainable system that works for all life on it. I am convinced of this. It's already begun to happen, all around the world."

THE TEN-PERCENT SOLUTION: A BRIEF SUMMARY

"It's *the ten-percent solution,* and it's a simple blueprint, a solution to both personal and global financial problems. It has two parts to it, *saving and tithing.*

"The first part is the solution to personal financial problems: *Save at least ten percent of your income until you have achieved financial independence.*

"The second part is the solution to a great many global problems: *Give ten percent of your income to worthy causes that help solve the world's problems in some way. And encourage ten percent of the individuals and corporations globally to give at least five to ten percent of their income to any programs they wish to support.*

"That's it. Even if it only solves ten percent of the world's problems, it'll still be a huge success."

THE FIRST PART OF THE TEN-PERCENT SOLUTION: SAVE TEN PERCENT OF YOUR INCOME

"The first part of the solution is nothing new. It's been

written about before — in *The Richest Man in Babylon,* for example — and certainly preached about before, but most people still haven't got it yet. And it's such a simple, *powerful* thing to do:

"*Save at least ten percent of your income.* Start now. Imagine you just got a ten percent pay cut, if that's what you have to do, and put away that ten percent. Even if you're in debt, like most people are, *start saving.*

"Better yet, think of a creative way to earn at least ten percent more income, and put that away. Start building a nest egg — put the money away for your future, for your financial independence. Keep saving at least ten percent of your income until you have enough to live off the interest and don't have to work.

"Most people think this is far-fetched, for some reason. And yet most people in this country make over a million dollars over the course of their working lives! Think about it! If you make an average of $30,000 a year for forty years, that's over a million dollars! It's, what? 1.2 million! If you saved ten percent of that, you'd have $120,000 principle, some of it building for forty years! If you can save $3,000 a year on the average, and you get, say, six percent return on it in a safe, conservative investment, after ten years you'd have... let's see...."

He paused for a moment, either remembering the number or calculating it mentally. "You'd have about $45,000. After twenty years, you have $120,000. After thirty years, you have $250,000. After forty years, you have almost half a million dollars.

"That's at only six percent interest. It's not at all that difficult to get a little education in investing and get an average of fifteen percent return, or more, a year. At fifteen percent interest, if you can manage to save $3,000 a year...." His head bobbed up and down; he looked like he was counting to himself. "You have $75,000 after ten years. After twenty years, you have $360,000. After thirty years, you have 1.5 million. After forty years, you have over 6 million dollars!

"In a few decades, most people can save enough so they can live off the interest on their savings. So it's not too far-fetched an idea, at all. It makes complete sense, in fact. And it snowballs through the generations: Once you do it, you leave much more to your heirs, and you help them do it.

"What if kids were taught to start saving ten percent from the time they started earning any money? They'd be wealthy by their thirties or forties!

"One of my granddaughters started saving ten percent of the money she earned for chores when she was ten. She just turned thirteen, and has a couple of hundred dollars earning interest. She still hasn't really grasped the concept, I don't think, but one day, if she continues, she'll realize she has a sizeable, growing chunk of capital that, eventually, *she can live off of.* And then she can do whatever she really wants to do with her life — unless she's been smart enough to do what she really wants all along, which is what I encourage everyone to do. Why wait for retirement? Why not start today, in whatever way you can?

"Start saving at least ten percent, and save until you have enough interest generated from that money to live off of it —

or until you have some other plan in place for your financial independence.

"I preach this to everyone around me. I told a friend of my wife's — a Brazilian woman — she should save ten percent of her income. She said, well, her mother and grandmother own several apartment buildings in Brazil that generate a lot of rental income and she was set to inherit enough to comfortably live on for the rest of her life. In that case, she didn't need to save ten percent — she already had her plan in place. But most of us aren't that fortunate. Most of us need to learn to save.

"Make it a priority. Pay yourself first. Tithe to yourself, to your future, to your family's future. For most people, it's best to have it automatically deducted from their paychecks, so they don't even notice it. That's what I did for years."

He looked at me and smiled, noticing how winded I was. He slowed the pace a bit, chuckling to himself. He obviously found it quite amusing that he was in better shape than I was.

"Eventually, your nest egg begins to grow. Then diversify it. Pick some good, solid stock and bond funds and stay with them. It's very satisfying to keep getting their reports, and watching it grow. In a few years, you have a good sum of money. In ten years, it's substantial. In twenty, you can see how you can live off the income those funds are generating.

"Don't plan on social security! Make your own plans, starting *today*. Save as much as you can through the company you work for — if you work for someone else — and save on your own as well.

"That's all there is to it — it's simple, it's effective. It's good for you, it's good for the economy. I don't know why more people don't do it."

"We're a nation of spenders, not savers," I said. I was speaking from experience.

"Well, we can change that," Bernie said. "It's for our own good. At least, we can become savers as well as spenders. It's not that hard to do — we're only talking *ten percent*. In fact, it's really fun to save, after a while. It becomes a great source of satisfaction, of security. Saving can become as habitual as spending. And it's a lot more rewarding in the long run — it leads to financial independence, where you can choose what you want to do with your life!

"This is a very nice state to attain, because then you naturally ask yourself, *What do I really want to do? What are my unique gifts? What can I do that no one else can do? What's my mission, my purpose in it all? What can I do to improve the quality of life on Earth?*

"And that leads right to the second part of the solution: the planetary solution."

We walked in silence. We came to the top of a knoll, and took in a view that swept over countless hills all the way to the distant mountains. I was breathing hard. Bernie hadn't even broken a sweat.

"Here, let's sit down. This is one of my favorite spots in

the whole world."

We sat in the grass at the crest of the knoll. The spot was matted, as if some person or animal often relaxed there. A light breeze cooled my head and chest. High cirrus clouds, brilliantly white, swept out like a thousand horses' tails in flight.

"It's gonna be a beautiful sunset," Bernie said. We sat and watched the clouds as they flew from west to east, running from the sun in a sky almost as dark blue as lapis.

THE SECOND PART OF THE SOLUTION: GIVE AWAY AT LEAST TEN PERCENT OF YOUR INCOME

"The second part of the solution has been known forever as well. It just hasn't been practiced widely enough. It's often called *tithing* — all it means is being generous, gratefully giving some back to the community, to the world.

"The first part of the ten-percent solution is doing the work necessary to support ourselves in the world. But the second part is the most important part — the Great Work — where we contribute to the world, in some way, and take care of at least one of the world's problems, in some form or other.

"We've seen, and maybe come to understand, that our beliefs are self-fulfilling. We've seen that our limiting beliefs — our fears and doubts — are not true in themselves: They become true, if you believe them. They become false when you grow beyond them, and come to see and believe that you are unique, and creative — ready, willing, and able to create what you want in life.

"If you believe you can, or if you believe you can't, you're right.

"By identifying our beliefs, and reaffirming the good ones and challenging the truth of the limiting ones, we change those old beliefs into more expansive beliefs, and our lives change, dramatically. I've seen this happen over and over.

"This is true globally as well as personally. Every society has its own set of inherent beliefs — about the nature of the individual, of their society, of the world. These beliefs change over time, as societies change, as the world changes, as people evolve. We're in a period where old beliefs are being challenged, globally, and are changing rapidly.

"There's a great book about this, called *The Chalice and the Blade*. Have you heard of it?"

"I've heard of it, but haven't read it."

"It's by Riane Eisler. She's brilliant. It's been called the most important book since Darwin's *Origin of Species*. Actually, I think it's more important than Darwin, because it proves — beyond a doubt — that our beliefs about society and the world were very different, even just a few thousand years ago — a tiny blip on the scale of human evolution. And, most important of all, it gives us a model for a livable future — based on going back to our roots, rather than inventing something new. It's the *partnership* model.

"All the world history we've been taught in school has

been the history of the *blade* — the history of what Eisler calls the *dominator* model — the conquest of warrior societies, beginning with the Greeks and Romans.

"Remember? World history — at least this is what I was taught — started somewhere in Sumer, 'the cradle of civilization', but quickly moved to Greece, where it all really started. Then it moved to Rome, then Europe, and finally America! Oh, China was mentioned somewhere as having an ancient culture. But all we ever learned about them was that they invented gun powder but only used it for fireworks, and never invented guns. Africa was 'the dark continent', shrouded in mystery. We knew little about it, except for Egypt, a great civilization 4,000 years ago. Latin America was hardly even mentioned in the world history I was taught. Australia was mentioned only as the place that was settled by British convicts.

"It was the story of conquerors. An endless procession of wars. That was what we were taught about our history.

"But Riane Eisler proves without a doubt that very different societies flourished before that, and have even coexisted with warrior societies, in some form, right into modern times — societies symbolized by the *chalice*, by partnership rather than domination. We need to study and emulate these partnership models of society, and apply them in every aspect of our lives — our families, our relationships, our businesses, our societies, our governments.

"This is how I see the Great Work ahead of us: the reinvention, the re-creation of society so it is built on *partnership* rather than domination. Partnership — from our families to the family of nations."

THE PROBLEM

"Everyone of us on Earth is aware of the major problems and challenges that face us. We all know what the problems are, at least the ones that affect us.

"People are starving in many parts of the world. People are homeless. People are crazy and desperate on the streets. People need psychological care, and help with chemical addictions — drugs and alcohol. A great many people — most of us, in fact, it could be argued — need therapy of one kind or another.

"People are hungry for an education of some kind, but don't have the resources to pay for it. The ideal of a free public school, from pre-school through college, has nearly evaporated.

"People who have received the education they need have dreams they want to fulfill. Artists want to be supported in their work. Business people want to be supported in their dreams. Those working for good causes need to be supported in their causes.

"People feel powerless to help other people, or protect animals or the environment in a meaningful way. That's the problem: our feeling of powerlessness. It leads to apathy and cynicism and selfishness. It leads nowhere. And it's based on a belief that's simply not true — we are far from powerless. Each one of us has a great deal of power, when we learn how to use it."

THE SOLUTION

"There's a widespread belief throughout the world today that there's a shortage of money. The belief is that there's not enough to go around. Somehow, the supply of money is limited, and it runs out. We're left in poverty — poverty in our thoughts and beliefs — and it leads to poverty of every kind.

"In reality, there's no shortage of money. It's exactly the same as it is with food — in fact, food and money are identical in many respects. You can exchange one for the other. And we all know there's plenty of food in the world. We pay farmers millions of dollars every year not to grow food. There's a distribution problem, however. The food isn't getting to the people who need it.

"There's plenty of money in the world, as well. It's sitting in huge piles all over the place, in cash, gold, stocks, bonds, real estate, inventory, art, jewelry. But there's a distribution problem. We're not getting enough money to the people who need it most.

"The solution is for a sufficient number of us — ten percent will do it — to distribute at least five to ten percent of our wealth around, on a regular basis. The solution is contained in the word *generosity*.

"And generosity leads to *generativity*. It generates more and more success in the world, more and more creative solutions. When generosity is linked to creativity, creative solutions can be found to the problems that face us.

"It's happening already. Generosity and creativity are flourishing, everywhere — the driving forces of a new age of partnership, global in scope, that has the potential to support everyone on the planet, and fulfill Buckminster Fuller's vision of a world with *a steadily improving standard of living for all, in a way that's entirely harmonious with all life on our Spaceship Earth.*

"We aren't wasting so many of our resources fighting each other any more. We aren't funding any major wars. We can invest huge amounts of capital into different resources that support *everyone* on every level of our society, worldwide. It's the surest, most humane way to world peace."

He fumbled around in his pockets and came up with a pen and a few sheets of folded-up paper. One page appeared to have affirmations or goals on it; another had twelve steps to something or other. But he folded them over and wrote on the back, first drawing a pyramid and then filling in words from the bottom to the top.

"Remember the work of Abraham Maslow, the psychologist? He taught that there's a pyramid of human consciousness — and people on every level of it need support and encouragement."

His drawing looked something like this:

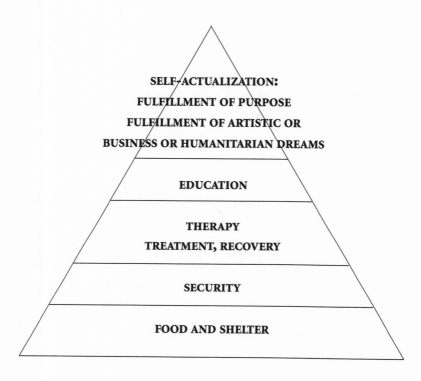

"The people on the bottom need food and shelter. If we don't have food and shelter, the activity of getting them takes all our time and energy. It dominates our consciousness.

"Once we have food and shelter, we need security. We need to protect ourselves, and the little we have. If we don't have security, the activity of getting it dominates our consciousness.

"Once we've attained at least a degree of security, we move up the pyramid and are able to focus on our immediate personal problems. We may need help in recovering from drug or alcohol abuse, or we may need therapy of some kind. Most of us lack confidence and self-esteem, most of us have a great many limiting core beliefs — almost all of us can benefit by spending some time in one kind of therapy or another.

"Once we've attained a certain amount of emotional stability, we move up into the realms of education. We find we're filled with questions, desires; we're driven to explore and learn. In the world of education, we discover our passion, and our focus. We discover what we want to do with our lives, and how to do it, and what we have to contribute to the world.

"Education is an endless, lifelong process, of course. But at a certain point almost all of us have some kind of artistic impulse, or business idea, or dream of helping others or the world in some way. We've found our vocation and learned the tools of our trade and want to apply our knowledge and do what we're here to do. Now we're at the top of the pyramid, at the stage Maslow called *self-actualization,* and we need to find creative ways to finance our artistic projects, and businesses, and humanitarian dreams. These are the challenges at the highest levels of the pyramid."

Bernie was positively exuberant, waving his arms like an orchestra conductor.

"From top to bottom, the core problem is a lack of money. For some reason, we've accepted the belief — on a global level — that there is a shortage of money. But a lot of people realize this belief is wrong, it's far too limited — *there is no shortage of money.* There's plenty of money in the world, just as there is plenty of *everything* in the universe. There's no shortage of money, there's only a distribution problem. We need to encourage those who have it to distribute it more effectively.

"We need to understand, and prove to ourselves, the generative power of giving. The result of the tithing of a large group of people — and corporations — is that people *globally* move up the pyramid.

"And that's the goal for all of us, individually and globally: to move up the pyramid and achieve our greatest fulfillment. Our purpose is to continue to evolve into something greater — as we have always done, and will continue to do."

He stared at the fast-moving clouds as they streaked across the sky. The entire dome of the heavens above us had turned into a brilliant light show of liquid gold and red flames weaving through chalky gray shadows. We both sat in silence. I had never seen a more beautiful sunset.

Bernie finally got up and stretched, reaching to the sky, then bent down to touch his toes. Then he did it again, in slow motion, taking a deep breath of air in as he reached up, and expelling the air noisily as he touched his toes.

He stood quietly for a few moments, watching the shape-shifting clouds. Then he said, "Let's head back." And he set out swiftly.

THE PARTNERSHIP MODEL:
THE NEXT STEP IN OUR EVOLUTION

When I caught up to him, he launched into his thoughts again:

"You know, we have the technology for an era of peace and prosperity. And we certainly have the motivation.

"And in so many ways, it's already begun. The Cold War is over. There is peace between the so-called superpowers. There hasn't been a world war in over fifty years. We've all seen how disastrous that course of action is for everyone, for all life on earth.

"There *is* a new renaissance that's beginning, still in its infancy. There are plenty of signs we're in a period of rapid growth. It begins with an evolution of consciousness, something that's been happening globally for a long time. There are millions of people out there today — scientists, teachers, writers, mothers, children, all kinds of people — who see it.

"Christ saw it, and taught us how to evolve, clearly, simply: *Love one another, as I have loved you . . . the Kingdom of Heaven is within.*

"Mother Teresa taught it, working with the poorest of the poor.

"Gandhi taught it, showing how powerful nonviolence can be politically.

"St. Francis taught it: *Lord make me an instrument of your peace . . . where there is anger, let me sow love.*

"Buddha taught it — we can attain serenity, beyond suffering, because the cause of our suffering is within us, within our attachment, our thirst for permanence.

"The *Vedas* of the Hindus teach it — *ahimsa*, nonviolence. I am that. That is all there is. I am one with the universe, so why would I do violence to myself?

"It's the partnership model. Practicing it brings us to a higher level of consciousness. We're evolving from the dominator model that has ruled the earth for 3,000 years or so into the partnership model that ruled for at least 30,000 years before that.

"It's struggling to be reborn. Yet it never was fully dominated. When Christ said, *Love your enemies,* he was planting the seeds of destruction of the system of domination — of course it can't stand in the face of love. The partnership model kept recurring, and will keep recurring forever, and will win out, because it's the ultimate power of the universe. It's the force of creation.

"Creation requires phenomenal partnership. The more we evolve, the more extensive that partnership is.

"Look at our bodies: Look at how many cells are working together, in perfect harmony. The heart cells are pumping blood cells all through our bodies. The liver cells are working together to filter out toxins. The cells in our eyes work together to give us sight! The brain cells are firing their hundred billion neural pathways and absorbing this information right now. Our bodies are a triumph of the partnership model of organization.

"Working in partnership with everyone makes sense. And we have the technology for an era of peace and plenty. We have the technology to feed the hungry, and house the homeless, and educate our children, and ourselves, so we all have the opportunity to realize our dreams.

"*We can have peace and plenty rather than war and poverty. The choice is up to us.* If we give at least ten percent of our income to the world, we can create an era of peace and plenty. I am convinced of that.

"And the best part of it is that it's already beginning to happen. The wheels are already in motion. *Forbes* magazine just did a big article on the new trend of the very rich — like Bill Gates and Warren Buffet — to give away their wealth to charities rather than leave it all to their families. It's far better for both their families and for the world.

"More and more, the private sector is realizing the government can't do it all, and is stepping in to contribute to their communities and the world. Companies are giving people paid vacations to do volunteer work, and taking on more and more special projects to support. George Bush's 'thousand points of light' can turn out to be more than just rhetoric, if we take this an important step further.

"As Riane Eisler puts it, we need to not only alleviate the impact of a system that's fundamentally imbalanced — a dominator system that constantly creates poverty, hunger, violence — we need to use a large portion of the ten percent we contribute to fund and encourage what Eisler calls new social and economic inventions — *partnership inventions.*

"We need, for example, economic inventions that give value to the most essential human work: caring and caretaking. Under the conventional economic systems, that work isn't counted — it's supposed to be done for free by women in male-controlled households. That's a dominator economic assumption. A partnership needs different economic assumptions. New assumptions are the first step, but we need practical ways of realizing them. And that's a huge challenge for us. Consciousness is the first step, but realizing it, practicing it, is the next necessary step." [6]

THE ONE PERCENT THAT CREATE THE SOLUTION

"In the sixties, the Maharishi — guru to the Beatles and Mia Farrow, you know," he said with a big smile, "The Maharishi said if just one percent of the population meditated, it would have an impact on the whole population. It seems to me that all of the positive changes of the sixties — and there were many, for minorities, gays, women, and the rest of us as well — all those changes were initiated when about one percent of the people began demanding them.

"Look at Vietnam, for example. I don't think there were more than one percent of us out there protesting the war, but it was enough. When Nixon saw half a million people gathered to protest, he caved in. He knew he had lost the support of the people.

"One percent is all it took. And that's all we need now. Get one percent of us imagining a better future, and doing something about it. Get one percent of us working on the solution, and our thoughts will spread like wildfire through the whole of humanity — and the solutions will appear.

"The process has already begun. These words are a tiny part of it. A vast network of people are already contributing, each in their own way, to a better world for all.

"It's a dream struggling to be born. And it's within our

power. We can all help the dream become a reality, each in our own way, according to the wishes of our hearts."

A HARBINGER

We walked on in silence. It had grown darker. Then Bernie stopped and pointed upward. The clouds flying over us had turned silver, and had formed two vast angel wings, with a perfect woman's form in between. It was so clear I had trouble for an instant believing I was seeing it. I wished I had a camera. My words will have to do:

She radiated, like a nebula, brilliantly lit by the moon hiding behind her. She was subtly multicolored, with reds and blues and purples, but mostly white and silver. The tips of her wings were luminescent. Her long robe swept out from her flight, and her jeweled crown shimmered with light. She had long windswept hair and, most amazing of all, a radiant face with absolutely clear, shining features.

She grew taller as her wings and body slowly and gracefully elongated. Then the cloud opened up, right in the middle, and a silver crescent moon appeared.

It was like witnessing a celestial birth — an image of immense beauty etched across a vast darkening sky.

Yes, there are angels watching over us, I found myself thinking. There are angels in our future, and a goddess of the moon. More and more of us are seeing how the feminine approach to life, the partnership approach, is the solution. We're all in this together. It's a lot more satisfying to be in partnership with everyone than to be in conflict. To be a lover, not a fighter. There are angels announcing a new age, just as there were angels announcing the birth of Christ — a harbinger of the endless rebirth of the partnership model of cooperation and love.

I don't know how long it lasted, how long we stood there. Maybe a minute. Maybe ten minutes.

Then it was gone, stretched into another form, and we walked on in silence.

THE KEY TO FULFILLMENT

When we got back to the house, Bernie said, "Let me get one more thing," and he disappeared down a hall and into his bedroom or office. He came back with a folded piece of paper.

"Here," he said. "Read it later."

He walked me out to my car. He didn't say a word. He was obviously absorbed in thought. Just before we reached my car, he stopped and said, "Let me try to sum it up briefly:

"The key to fulfillment, to a wonderful life, is to do what's in your heart, and to put your heart into what you do. Then you'll succeed. Always.

"It's in our language: we have a fire in our belly . . . or we don't have the heart for it. Combine the wishes and dreams in your heart with the fire in your belly — your *power* — and you'll create what you want, what you desire, what you *intend*.

"The key to becoming *completely* fulfilled is to *serve people with love.*

"If you're in the restaurant business, you're serving food to people. And food is a form of love. You're serving love. Now make sure you're serving *with* love.

"If you're a parent, if you're a child, if you're an artist, if you're in business, the solution to *all* problems is found somewhere in *the partnership model* — in serving people with love, in partnership with them."

He gave me a warm smile, then turned and walked away.

His walk slowed to a stop, then he turned around and came back.

YOU HAVE ALL THE TOOLS
YOU NEED WITHIN

"I've said all I need to say. You have all the tools you need now. Don't forget — all of the tools are *within you.* Your success doesn't depend on anything outside yourself, in the world. Your success depends on your vision.

"Powerful people are not at the mercy of outside forces beyond their control; powerful people create their own success as a result of their focused vision and consistent action toward it.

"We're here for a great purpose. We all sense it, we all know it's true. And yet so many of us find ourselves, day after day, year after year, doing things that aren't serving us or anyone else, things that aren't aligned with our purpose.

"The Tibetans have a tremendous epic poem about a hero named Gesar. He was chosen by the gods for a great mission in life: to overcome four demon kings who were intent on destroying Buddhism. He overcame the first king, but then settled down with the king's wife and lived in satisfied luxury and forgot his great mission. After six years, the gods had to come to Gesar and remind him to get on with his great work.

"We're all like Gesar, to some degree. We're here to accomplish something great, but we've settled down into comfortable old habits and keep postponing our great work for another day.

"Every day, you have the power to do *something* aligned with your vision and purpose. Do it. Do it now."

He spoke with passion, as if to a large imaginary crowd.

"Every moment, we have a choice. Choose to do the things that are aligned with your vision and purpose, rather than all those things that keep you stuck in old habits, old beliefs.

"*I challenge you to be great.* You'll do it only by envisioning greatness, and taking the first steps toward it. You have all the tools you need, but it's up to you to put them to use.

"You have all the time you need; you have all the power you need. There are no more acceptable excuses. You can't whine anymore, or make believe you're a victim. You can no longer believe you're powerless, suffering the results of forces beyond your control. Now you know the truth, and you can't hide from it: You're a powerful, creative person, and you have a mission to do. You intuitively know — you've always known — what that mission is.

"Get on with it! Greatness is within your vision. It's within your grasp."

He smiled and turned and ambled back to his house, gazing at the silver night sky.

AFTERWORD

And though I have the gift of prophecy, and understand all mysteries, and all knowledge...and have not charity, I am nothing.

— I Corinthians 13:2

I drove home in silence, remembering. Images and words came back to me.

I forgot about the piece of paper he had given me until I undressed for bed and noticed it sticking out of my back pocket. It was handwritten in broad strokes, with a few lines inserted that he had apparently added later:[7]

Thoughts upon a rainy Sunday

When I think back
  on the good times, and the hard times,
    the struggles, and the joys,
  I think of the times that were the most
    meaningful in life
The times that were most worthwhile
And those were the moments of love,
    giving, and laughter
  The moments of joy and fun
Playing with a child,
  A silent sunset
Telling my mother I loved her
    Watching the wind blow through
    a eucalyptus tree in a storm

Standing alone in a church
    Awestruck alone on a mountainside
Singing O Mistress Mine to a maiden
    hidden in a forest
Embracing a loved one
  Drenched in sweat
    Listening to a friend read Tolkien
      under a white cedar tree in the woods
    Watching Javanese puppets all night long
Gazing at the stars, the endless stars
    Sixteen meteorites in one evening
And an angel in the clouds
    Giving birth to a crescent moon

The worthwhile moments had nothing to do with
  fears, doubt, sadness, angst,
    pain, guilt, cynicism,
      existential suffering
The worthwhile moments are the Zen moments
  When I'm fully in the present
    Enjoying, loving
  And simply being
    Without a thought of yesterday or tomorrow

I must remember this
  And live my present in this way
Forgetting fear and doubt
  Finding delight in the moment
    Seeing the light in the moment
It's such a simple thing to do
  Every child knows it. . . .

And on the back of the paper, he had written:

And though I have the gift of prophecy, and
understand all mysteries, and all knowledge;
and though I have all faith, so that I could
remove mountains, and have not charity, I am
nothing.

— I Corinthians 13:2

TEN KEYS TO TRANSFORM
YOUR LIFE AND THE WORLD

1) Imagine your ideal scene.
2) Discover your vocation, and your mission or purpose in life.
3) Create long-term goals — at least a five-year plan, that will evolve into a lifetime plan.
4) Create short-term goals that move you toward each long-term goal.
5) Visualize your success.
6) Learn to face your emotions, and see the gift in each one.
7) Practice the fine art of communication.
8) Listen to the voice of your intuition.
9) Practice the fine art of detachment.
10) Give abundantly and reap the rewards — be part of the ten-percent solution to personal and global financial problems.

NOTES

1. From *As You Think* by James Allen (New World Library, 1987), pp. 39-40.

2. Many of these core beliefs are reprinted, with permission, from *The Creative Visualization Workbook* by Shakti Gawain (New World Library, revised edition 1995), pp. 48-51.

3. The core belief process was first published in *The Creative Visualization Workbook,* pp. 51-54.

4. From *A Two-Second Love Affair* by Marc Allen (New World Library, 1995), p. 56.

5. From *Letters to My Son* by Kent Nerburn (New World Library, 1994), p. 51.

6. From Riane Eisler's work in progress on Partnership Economics. Reprinted with permission.

7. From *A Two-Second Love Affair* by Marc Allen (see above), p. 49.

ACKNOWLEDGMENTS

First I must thank Kent Nerburn for giving me permission to steal a certain part of this story so blatantly from his great book, *Neither Wolf nor Dog.* I'm shameless. I apologize. I just couldn't resist.

And I'd like to acknowledge those who inspired this book:

Bernie Nemerov, for believing in me;

Shakti Gawain, for *Creative Visualization,* and for living every moment with absolute honesty and integrity;

Riane Eisler, for *The Chalice and the Blade,* and for showing us it's possible to live with the chalice instead of the blade;

Barbara Marx Hubbard, for *Conscious Evolution,* her vision of a harmonious, cooperative future, and for her loving spirit;

Buckminster Fuller, for his vision of a world that can work for everyone;

Abraham Maslow, for his understanding of the pyramid of human consciousness;

Deepak Chopra, for his understanding of East and West, old and new, and for saying a phrase that sums up this book: *Within every desire is the seed and mechanics of its fulfillment;*

James Allen, for *As You Think,* a masterpiece;

Catherine Ponder, for her books, and especially her affirmation, *in an easy and relaxed manner, in a healthy and positive way, in its own perfect time;*

Professor Arya, from the University of Minnesota, for his instruction in yoga and meditation;

Swami Satchidananda, for saying, *Make no appointments, and you won't have any disappointments;*

Katsuki Sekida, for teaching Zen meditation to a bunch of clueless Americans, and for writing *Zen Training;*

Tarthang Tulku, for the ancient teachings from Tibet, and for his understanding of *skillful means* — and for trying to keep a bunch of wild Americans in their rooms at night meditating rather than "running around here and there";

Ken Keyes Jr., for modernizing the ancient teachings so well and understanding the seven centers of consciousness — and making it okay to run around here and there so much;

Thich Nhat Hanh, for teaching it all so serenely.

And I shouldn't fail to mention some others who inspired me and changed the course of my life: John Clarke Donahue, Tony Steblay, Danny Campbell, Carol Swardson, Syd Walter, Marlowe Hotchkiss, Norah Holmgren, Collin Wilcox, Kimberley Horne, Will Donicht, Sharon Scandur;

And Joe Durepos and Jason Gardner, who contributed so much to this book, and Becky Benenate, who has contributed so much to New World Library;

And Auri Nogueira, an incarnation of the goddess...as every woman is, for the goddess comes in an infinite number of forms....

Thank you, each and every one.

BIBLIOGRAPHY &
RECOMMENDED READING

As You Think by James Allen (New World Library, 1987).

The Chalice and the Blade by Riane Eisler (HarperSan Francisco, 1988).

Conscious Evolution by Barbara Marx Hubbard (New World Library, 1997).

Creating Affluence by Deepak Chopra (New World Library/Amber-Allen, Publishing 1993).

Creating True Prosperity by Shakti Gawain (New World Library, 1997).

Creative Visualization by Shakti Gawain (New World Library, 1995).

Don't Sweat the Small Stuff by Richard Carlson (Hyperion, 1997).

Embracing Each Other: Relationship as Teacher, Healer & Guide by Hal and Sidra Stone (Nataraj Publishing, 1993).

Embracing Our Selves: The Voice Dialogue Manual by Hal and Sidra Stone (Nataraj Publishing, 1993).

The Handbook to Higher Consciousness by Ken Keyes, Jr.
(Love Line Books, 1983).

Illusions by Richard Bach (Dell, 1989).

Letters to a Young Poet by Rainer Maria Rilke (New World
Library, 1992).

Letters to My Son by Kent Nerburn (New World Library,
1994).

Living in the Light by Shakti Gawain (Nataraj Publishing,
1986).

The Seven Spiritual Laws of Success by Deepak Chopra (New
World Library/Amber-Allen Publishing, 1995).

*Tantra for the West: Everyday Miracles and Other Tools for
Transformation* by Marc Allen (New World Library,
1992).

A Two-Second Love Affair by Marc Allen (New World Library,
1995).

Visionary Business: An Entrepreneur's Guide to Success by
Marc Allen (New World Library, 1995).

You Can Be Happy No Matter What by Richard Carlson (New
World Library, 1997).

ABOUT THE AUTHOR

Marc Allen is president and co-founder (with Shakti Gawain) of New World Library. He has written several books, including *Visionary Business — An Entrepreneur's Guide to Success* and a book of poetry, *A Two-Second Love Affair*. He has also written several albums of music, including *Breathe*, *Petals*, and *Solo Flight*.

He lives with his family in Northern California.

Made in the USA
Lexington, KY
21 November 2011